Basic Quiltmaking Techniques

for Divided Circles

Sherry Reis

Martingale
& COMPANY

Bothell, Washington

Credits

President . . . . Nancy J. Martin
CEO/Publisher . . . . Daniel J. Martin
Associate Publisher . . . . Jane Hamada
Editorial Director . . . . Mary V. Green
Technical Editor . . . . Christine Barnes
Design and Production Manager . . Cheryl Stevenson
Copy Editor . . . . Tina Cook
Text Designer . . . . Kay Green
Illustrator . . . . Lisa McKenney
Photographer . . . . Brent Kane

Basic Quiltmaking Techniques
for Divided Circles
© 1998 by Sherry Reis

Martingale & Company
PO Box 118
Bothell, WA 98041-0118 USA

Printed in the United States of America
03 02 01 00 99 98   6 5 4 3 2 1

Library of Congress Cataloging-in-Publication Data
Reis, Sherry
        Basic quiltmaking techniques for divided circles / Sherry Reis.
        p. cm.
        Includes bibliographical references.
        ISBN 1-56477-238-1
        1. Patchwork—Patterns. 2. Quilting—Patterns. I. Title.
TT835.R453 1998
746.46'041—dc21   98-24783
                                             CIP

Dedication

To Carol Doak, with love and gratitude for her endless gift of an extraordinary friendship. We will always be "forever friends."

Acknowledgments

I would like to extend my genuine appreciation to:

My husband, Tom, my son, Andy, and my daughter, Nina, for their constant love and for allowing me the freedom to realize my dream.

My quilting pals: Colleen, Jane, Martha, Joanie, Paulette, Sue, Lynne, Joan, Shirley, Amy, Cindy, Susie, Cheryl, and Carol for their friendship, encouragement, and support, and all the good times on the second Thursday; Jamie, Wendy, Joan, and Beth for their telephone hugs and notes of cheer—always when I needed them.

Marion Shelton for her warm and gracious introduction to Martingale and Company.

Ursula Reikes for her incredible expertise, her patience, and her calming voice.

Mrs. Betty Walters, who taught me which end of the needle to hold and more.

Christine Barnes for her skillful editing and the warm working relationship we shared during the production of this book.

Donna Shore for gladly sharing her mother's sewing machine way back when.

Jacque Hanks for opening my eyes to the world of quiltmaking.

Carol Clements, my friend and neighbor, who always finds at least fifteen minutes to help.

My sisters, Doe and Marj, for all the things I too often take for granted, like always being there.

Finally, in memory of my parents, Barton and Miriam Cressy, for teaching me all the valuable lessons of life and, most of all, for their unconditional love.

MISSION STATEMENT

WE ARE DEDICATED TO PROVIDING QUALITY PRODUCTS AND SERVICE BY WORKING TOGETHER TO INSPIRE CREATIVITY AND TO ENRICH THE LIVES WE TOUCH.

Table of Contents

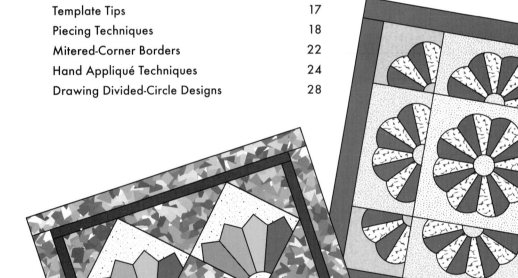

Foreword

It has been nearly twenty years since Sherry and I sat side-by-side in our basic quiltmaking classes. We were "newbies" but eager to learn how to make patchwork quilts. Every week was an adventure as we absorbed each new quiltmaking technique.

To this day, I vividly remember being impressed with the technique of dividing a circle, because it solved the mystery of the Grandmother's Fan, Dresden Plate, and Mariner's Compass blocks I so admired. That early learning experience has served both Sherry and me in our later quiltmaking endeavors.

I am thrilled that Sherry is going to show you how to create patchwork based on the divided circle. The information in these pages will lead you down the road to new patchwork adventures and open creative doors in your quiltmaking.

Sherry has made some wonderful quilts based on divided circles and taught many others the secrets of these methods. Now you have the chance to expand your basic quiltmaking knowledge as Sherry carefully guides you through the steps for creating patchwork based on divided circles.

When you are ready to explore creative options, Sherry's step-by-step procedures for drawing divided-circle designs will give you the tools you need to create your own block patterns.

Enjoy and have fun!

Carol Doak

Preface

If anyone had told me that first night I attended a beginning quilting class that I would one day be sitting at a computer writing a book on techniques for quiltmaking, the echoes of my laughter would still be heard. My intention in taking those first classes was to learn how to make quilts. As my friend and I sat in class week after week, we were introduced to various techniques that became the foundation of our quiltmaking knowledge. Once my interest was captured (by the end of the first evening), I embarked on a journey that has been both fulfilling and rewarding.

Along the way, as my appetite for quiltmaking information grew, I fed my "what's next?" curiosity by taking classes, reading, and experimenting. Eventually, I began teaching to share what I had learned with others. Each step has been a challenge with positive results.

One class I offer teaches students how to draw quilt blocks in any size to make patchwork templates. At the conclusion of one class, a student inquired, "How do you draw circular designs?" With that simple question, I arrived on the doorstep of this book.

You may be new to quiltmaking, or perhaps you have quilted for a while and are just new to divided circles. In any case, good for you for expanding your knowledge of the art! Had I not continued to challenge myself with new techniques and concepts after that initial quilting class, who knows where either of us would be right now. Welcome to the circle! What do you say we give it a spin?

Introduction

If you are familiar with *Your First Quilt Book (or it should be!)* by Carol Doak, you are off to a great start. Carol not only provided you with the quiltmaking information necessary for beginning projects, but she also helped build your confidence, and in the process you had fun. If you continued the series with *Basic Quilt-making Techniques for Hand Appliqué* by Mimi Dietrich, you added to your knowledge as Mimi helped you acquire the skills needed for hand appliqué. Feel free to refer to these books, as often as necessary, for we will use their lessons and combine them with divided-circle techniques to expand your quiltmaking experience.

The patchwork in *Basic Quiltmaking Techniques for Divided Circles* is based on a circle that has been divided into equal sections or wedges. Picture a pie (your favorite flavor). Restaurants use a wheel-like tool to slice their pies. When pressed into the pie, this tool cuts equalsized pieces. Imagine your pie cut in this fashion. Are you getting the idea?

Now imagine a fabric circle. Just like a pie, you can divide the circle into pieces to make a number of traditional quilt-block designs. To construct a divided-circle block, you will need templates. In this book, I provide the necessary templates for six projects. For those of you interested in designing your own projects, I also provide simple, step-by-step lessons that show you how to divide circles to create templates.

Because the technique for divided circles is different from other quiltmaking techniques, you will need to learn some new terms. Additional tools will come into play when you are ready for the mechanics of the technique.

Each of the included projects gives you the opportunity to use both hand and machine skills. All appliqué will be worked by hand using your favorite method, while most of the piecing can be completed by hand or machine. If you generally use one method over the other, now is your chance to expand your skills.

Are you feeling like the new kid on the block? Let me introduce you to three symbols and tell you what they mean:

Tip boxes include handy hints that will make a process or technique a bit easier. Read these right away!

Alert boxes let you know when you need to be careful. Your guardian angel will alert you so you don't make a common mistake.

Down the Road boxes contain information that will come in handy on future patchwork projects, after you have more quiltmaking experience. You don't need this information right away, though, so feel free to ignore the Down the Road boxes until you're ready to explore further.

When I try something for the first time, I find it useful to get an overview of the subject. For that reason, I recommend you read all the information in this book before beginning the projects. It won't take long, and you will begin with confidence and the knowledge needed for a successful experience. Enjoy it all. I can't wait to see the results!

Coming to Terms with the Divided Circle

Do any of these terms ring a bell?—appliqué, bias, block, borders, piecing, seam allowance, appliqué stitch, and glue basting. They do? Yea team! Even if you needed to sneak a peek at *Your First Quilt Book (or it should be!)*, it still counts. You can apply these and other terms you already know to divided circles. There are, however, some terms unique to the divided-circle technique.

Arc: A portion of the curved line that creates a circle.

Arc

Wedge: A section of a circle that consists of an arc (the wide, curved portion of the shape) and two straight lines on each end of the arc that narrow to the center of the circle.

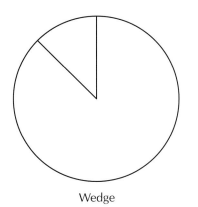

Wedge

Ray: A wedge that radiates from the center of a circle. The widest portion is toward the center, with the point facing out.

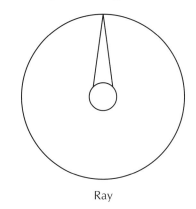

Ray

Dividing Lines: Vertical, horizontal, and diagonal lines that run through the center of a circle, connecting opposite sides. These lines divide a circle into equal sections.

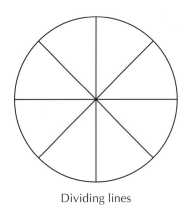

Dividing lines

Smooth Edge: The arc edge of a wedge with no embellishment. Sometimes known as a "plain edge."

Smooth edge

Rounded Edge: The arc edge of the wedge embellished with a circular shape to create a scalloped look.

Rounded edge

Pointed Edge: The arc edge of the wedge drawn to a point at the center. Sometimes known as a "fancy point." The sharpness of the point can vary.

Pointed edge

Diagonal Edge: The arc edge of the wedge drawn to a point at one side along a single diagonal line.

Diagonal edge

Concentric Circles: Various-sized circles having a common center point. Think of a target.

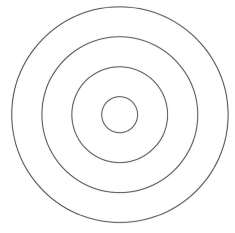

Concentric circles

Tools for the Divided-Circle Mechanic

You will be pleased to know that you already own most of the tools and supplies needed for the divided-circle technique. Listed below are some tools required for drawing divided-circle designs.

Compass: Use this instrument to draw circles. There are many types of compasses, ranging from the ones you used for math class, to drafting compasses, to the yardstick variety.

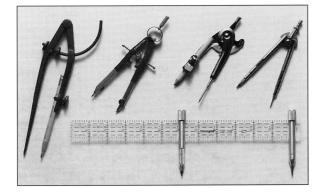

There are several points to consider when purchasing your compass:
• The compass must hold its setting. If the setting fluctuates as you draw, the compass will not produce a true circle.
• Attaining the setting should not be difficult. If it takes great effort to reach the desired setting, the compass is not working properly.
• Make sure the maximum distance the compass can reach is great enough to fit your needs.

It's okay to start with an inexpensive compass and use it as long as it continues to work efficiently. When you feel the need to move up in quality, invest in a better compass.

Don't use the compass left at home by your son or daughter. Chances are it no longer holds its settings, and that is why it has been left behind.

Drawing Rulers: These were designed for those of us who can't draw a straight line. Kidding aside, good drawing rulers are a step up from the wooden or colored plastic ones we used in school. They are see-through plastic and are marked in inches or centimeters, or are gridded. The ones marked in inches or centimeters generally start at a 0 marking that is about ¼" from the left end of the ruler. The last inch marking is about ¼" from the right end of the ruler. With this feature, even if your ruler wears slightly from normal use, your first and last inches will still be accurate. You can find this ruler in most office-supply stores.

The gridded ruler is a 2" x 18" clear-plastic ruler marked with a ⅛" grid (usually in red or blue). The inch markings are located on each long edge. Sewing centers often carry this ruler.

If you use a rotary ruler for drawing, the chance for error is great. The thick ruler often casts a shadow, making it difficult to draw a line exactly where you want it. Likewise, never use a thin, plastic drawing ruler for a rotary ruler. You are likely to ruin the ruler or, worse yet, cut yourself.

Protractor: A plastic half-circle marked to measure degrees. I use this tool to verify the accuracy of my templates. A protractor is not a "must have," but it comes in handy. Resist the temptation to use the ones your children have discarded. If you want a protractor, buy one that is of better quality.

Mechanical Pencil: This is the pencil you never need to sharpen, yet the line it produces is always the same size. A mechanical pencil really helps maintain accuracy in your drawing. Although it costs more than a wooden pencil, it won't break your piggy bank and is worth the expense.

Everybody loves shiny new tools. At the risk of sounding selfish, if you value your new purchases and you live with someone who thinks they are really neat, reach an understanding about their use. If all else fails, hide your good tools. Who needs the frustration of reaching for a compass only to discover it went to school?

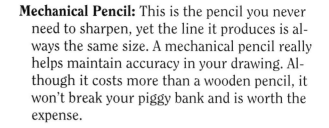

Introduction to the Divided Circle

Most traditional patchwork is based on the grid system, which divides a square into an equal number of units across and down. Additional lines within the grid create the shapes for your patchwork.

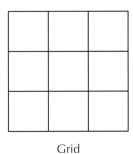

Grid

Divided-circle patchwork begins with a circle instead of a square. It, too, needs lines to divide it into equal sections. The sections are created by drawing vertical, horizontal, and diagonal lines that run through the center point and connect opposite sides of the circle. These are known as "dividing lines." Once divided, the sections resemble pieces of a pie or have a wedge shape. These wedges or sections are all equal. If you choose, you can further divide these shapes to create thinner wedges.

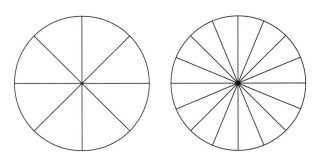

If you draw a smaller circle in the center of the original divided circle, look what happens. There are still eight sections, but they now look as though someone has taken a bite out of the pointed end of each wedge. The sections are still equal.

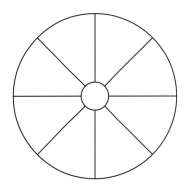

Perhaps you want to alter the arc portion of the wedges to make a more attractive shape. Say it with me, "The sections are still equal."

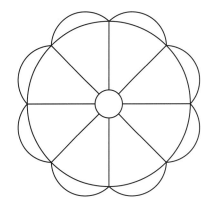

When you divide one wedge, you must divide them all, or they won't be equal. Therefore, when you divide four equal wedges, you end up with eight equal wedges. When you divide eight equal wedges, you end up with sixteen equal wedges, and so on.

For divided circles the motto is: All wedges must be created equal.

Let me show you several blocks produced with the divided-circle technique. The first two, Grandmother's Fan and Dresden Plate, are no doubt familiar to you.

When you look at the Grandmother's Fan block, are you scratching your head and thinking "I don't get it—where is the circle?" The Grandmother's Fan block is one-fourth of a circle.

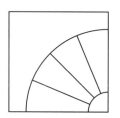

Grandmother's Fan

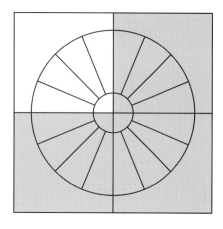

A Dresden Plate block is made up of a whole circle.

Dresden Plate

Let's take a look at other possibilities of the divided-circle framework.

If you draw additional lines to connect the eight dividing lines, look what happens:

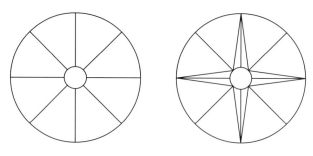

Once again, you end up with wedge shapes, but they are turned around, and the arc portion of the wedge is now concave (curving inward) instead of convex (curving outward). Or, to put it another way, the "bite" has been taken from the widest end. These wedges appear to radiate from the center circle. For that reason, we call them "rays."

If you draw lines to connect the dividing lines of two rays to the dividing line between them, look what happens. You have created a new design, a simple Mariner's Compass block.

Mariner's Compass

You can now add Mariner's Compass to the list of blocks created with the divided-circle technique.

Now that you are familiar with the basic concepts of divided circles, the relationship between Grandmother's Fan blocks, Dresden Plate blocks, and Mariner's Compass blocks should be clear to you. Consider yourself formally introduced to the divided-circle family.

Not all Mariner's Compass blocks look the same or are as simple as the one shown on the facing page. They do, however, have characteristics in common:
- All have rays that originate from a common center.
- All are created by using the divided-circle technique.

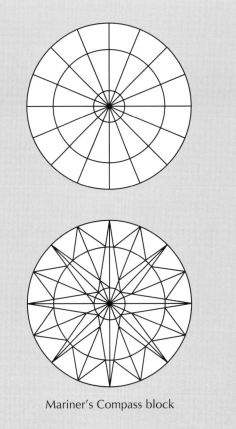

Mariner's Compass block

What changes the appearance of the Mariner's Compass block?
- The number of equal divisions (wedges) in the circle. In the preceding illustration there are eight. You could change that to sixteen, thirty-two, or more. Keep in mind that the more divisions there are, the smaller the sections become.
- The addition of one or more concentric circles between the outer circle and the center circle. The wedges remain equal. If you were to stack them one on top of the next, they would still be identical. Now, however, each wedge will be scored with an added arc or arcs between the two original circles.
- The addition of connecting lines. If you make more divisions and add another circle or circles, you create many more places for the lines to connect.

Let's use an example. If your circle has sixteen divisions and one added concentric circle, the divided-circle framework looks like the upper illustration. When you add connecting lines, you create the Mariner's Compass block.

Techniques for Divided Circles

You may be new to this technique, but give yourself some credit: you already have some quiltmaking experience. If you've read the other books in the Basic Quiltmaking Techniques series, you know how to select fabrics for a project, piece patchwork by hand or machine, and hand appliqué. Perhaps you even have a completed project or two under your belt. Don't look now, but I think you've become a quilter. (How do you know when you've become a quilter? Your college student's closet has become home to your fabric stash, you order cable television just to get "Simply Quilts," and you learn that UFO really stands for "unfinished object.")

I don't want to take the space to go over information you already know or can look up, unless it is important to the divided-circle technique or it will help you use this book. The application of divided circles to quiltmaking creates new design opportunities. These design opportunities will be our focus in the coming pages.

Fabrics in the Round

Is anyone having a fabric attack? Here we are on page 14, and I've hardly mentioned fabric. No one loves fabric more than I do (just ask my husband). So let's go.

Let's talk first about the aspects of fabric you must consider when working with divided-circle designs. In these designs, wedge shapes replace squares and rectangles. If you compare a wedge to a square, it's not surprising that the shapes relate differently to fabric. Here are some key points to consider:

Grain Lines

The first consideration is a single word that strikes fear in the hearts of beginning quiltmakers —bias. No matter how you approach divided circles, you will always have a bias edge somewhere—there is no getting around it. The bias grain has the greatest stretch; therefore, you must take extra care when handling the wedges and rays so their shapes won't distort. Otherwise, your piecing will not be accurate.

When marking template shapes on your fabric, be sure to use a sandpaper marking board. To make one, just glue a piece of fine-grade sandpaper to a file folder. The sandpaper grips the fabric, minimizing the stretch and maximizing the accuracy of your marking.

Let's experiment by placing a wedge-shaped template on a piece of fabric. If you place the template so the straight grain of the fabric runs through the center of the wedge, all edges will be on the bias. When you join two wedges, the edges will both be on the bias. These edges are much more likely to stretch than straight-grain edges.

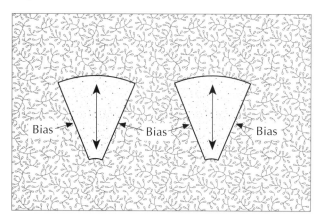

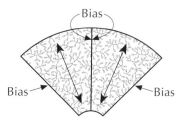

To avoid this problem, place the wedge template on your fabric so the straight grain is parallel to one of the long edges. This wedge will have one edge on the straight grain and one edge on the bias grain. If you match a straight-grain edge to a bias edge when you join the wedges, the straight-grain edge will stabilize the bias edge.

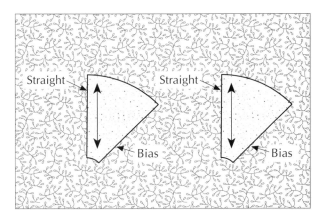

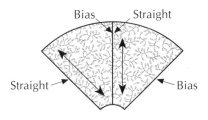

It looks as though we have found a way to eliminate at least some bias edges, but wait, here comes that pesky word "except." Having one template edge on the straight grain works beautifully, except in certain circumstances.

Directional and Stripe Fabrics

Directional and stripe fabrics can be very effective in divided circles. Generally, they are most appealing when

- stripes run on the vertical or horizontal straight-grain line, or
- directional fabrics run on the vertical straight-grain line.

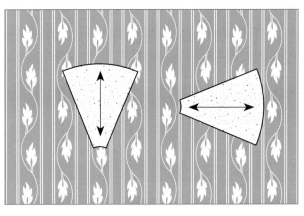

Stripe

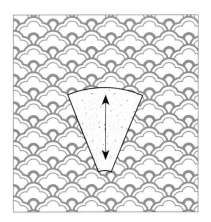

Directional

What does this all boil down to? To use these fabrics to their best advantage, cut the wedges so the straight grain runs through the center of the wedge. Your edges will all be bias edges. This really isn't a problem; you just need to be aware of the consequences.

You will not be wrong if you place one long edge of the wedge on the straight grain of these fabrics; it is strictly a matter of personal preference. Look at the "Grandmother's Fan Pillow" (page 35). The second wedge from the left is made from a stripe fabric cut with one long edge on the straight grain.

Centering a Design Element

Perhaps you have a truly magnificent fabric with a gorgeous floral element. It occurs to you that the element would be spectacular centered in each of your wedges. This kind of placement is easier than you think.

Grain really isn't the issue, because it is only possible to have one edge of the wedge on the straight grain. Our goal is to place the element in exactly the same spot in each wedge.

If you're not familiar with the difference between hand-piecing and machine-piecing templates, turn to page 47 and look at an example. A hand-piecing template shows the finished line, without a seam allowance around the edges, while a machine-piecing template includes a ¼"-wide seam allowance. Now, with that bit of knowledge, let's try the following method for centering a design element:

1. Trace the machine-piecing template onto a sheet of template plastic. To see what the finished wedge will look like, also trace the hand-piecing template ¼" inside the first line. Do not trace the grain arrow. Cut out the template.

Wedge template

Not all pencils and pens mark well on all template plastics. Test to make sure that yours will.

2. Place the template on the right side of the fabric and move it until the desired element appears within the hand-piecing lines as you wish. This is how the wedge will look when completed. Without moving the template, trace the element onto the template plastic.

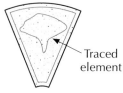

Traced element

3. Match the tracing on the template to the element in the fabric. Mark and cut as many wedges as you need.

How frequently an element appears in a fabric, or the distance between the elements, may make it necessary to buy additional fabric. Determine how many wedges you need and buy enough fabric to give you that many elements. You will certainly be disappointed if your piece of fabric contains only seven elements when you need eight—and the quilt store just closed.

Normally, you don't mark on the right side of fabric, but in order to match the template tracing to the fabric element, you must be able to see it. Since the template includes the ¼"-wide seam allowance, you can cut the fabric on the pencil line. If you are hand piecing, you must add the pencil lines needed. (Don't forget to use the sandpaper board.)

At the risk of sounding like a nag, be careful when adding hand-piecing lines. Once the wedge shape is cut, there is no longer anything to keep the bias edge stable. Even with the sandpaper board, you can easily stretch those edges. Be careful and mark gently.

If all this talk has left you feeling the need to get up-close-and-personal with some fabric, take a break and visit your local quilt shop. It surely has something new to delight you.

Template Tips

You already know that a template is what you use to trace a patchwork shape onto fabric. Templates made from template plastic are the most durable.

As we discussed on the facing page, hand-piecing templates are the finished size of the piece. For these, you must add ¼"-wide seam allowances when you cut fabric pieces. Machine-piecing templates include the ¼" seam allowances. With these, you cut on the traced pencil line. On machine-piecing templates, you must also mark the finished-line points.

This book includes templates you can use for hand piecing or machine piecing. Templates with curved edges (Templates A, B, C, D, E, and G) obviously cannot be cut with rotary equipment. For curved shapes, consider the following methods:

Hand-Piecing Templates for Wedge Shapes

1. Make a hand-piecing template.
2. Trace the template onto your fabric.
3. Using scissors, cut the curved edge ¼" from the pencil line. You don't need to measure the distance, just estimate.

When estimating the ¼" seam allowance, it's best to be generous and trim the excess after stitching. Underestimating could result in a scant seam allowance that frays or pulls out once appliquéd.

4. Rotary cut the straight edges ¼" from the pencil line.

Machine-Piecing Templates for Wedge Shapes

1. Make the machine-piecing template, including the seam allowances. Mark the points where the finished-size lines intersect.
2. Use a ⅛" hole punch to make a hole in the template at each point.
3. Trace the template onto the wrong side of your fabric and mark the fabric through the holes.
4. Using scissors, cut on the pencil lines.

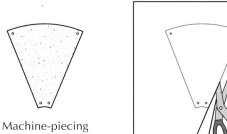

Machine-piecing template with holes

Your method of appliqué may depend on pencil lines. If it does and you are using the machine-piecing template, follow these steps.

1. Make the hand-piecing template.
2. Place it ¼" inside the pencil lines on your fabric piece, matching the points to the dots on the fabric.
3. Trace the curved edges.

Here are a few extra tips to make your work with templates easier:

• Template G is a circle and must be appliquéd. For that reason, it is provided as a hand-piecing template only.

• The points on the machine-piecing templates in this book are extremely important. Be sure to mark them on your templates and use them as directed: For Templates A, B, C, D, and E, you will stitch between the points. For Templates H, I, J, and K, the points are for matching purposes; you will stitch through them. For Template L, both hand and machine piecers will use the center dot for matching.

• Templates A, B, and E each have two straight-of-grain arrows on them. Refer to "Grain Lines" (page 14) to select which arrow to use.

Finally, you are ready to make the templates of your choice.

Piecing Techniques

You may be smiling to yourself right now and thinking, "I know all about piecing. I'm in good shape here." Well, guess what? You're probably right. If you have any quiltmaking experience, whether it's by hand or machine, you are familiar with basic piecing techniques. There is, however, an important point that I must repeat: Accuracy in piecing is essential! Your ¼" seam allowances *must* be true. Precision will pay off, and your finished projects will prove it.

Piecing techniques vary a bit with the projects. If the block has wedges, you will be joining identical shapes. If you are making a Mariner's Compass project, you will be joining different shapes, some of them asymmetrical. On the following pages, you will find information for both hand and machine piecing. Read the section that applies to you. You will be up and running—make that sitting and piecing—in no time at all.

Wedges

Hand Piecers

You are ahead of the game here. When you piece wedges, you begin and end with a backstitch at the point where the pencil lines intersect. (This technique keeps the curved-edge seam allowance free for appliqué). As a hand piecer, you already do that. See how easy that was?

Machine Piecers

"Template Tips" (page 17) instructed you to mark the points on your machine-piecing templates, make a hole at each point, and mark dots on your fabric through the holes. These dots are important because you will stitch between them. Follow these steps:

1. Place 2 wedges right sides together.
2. Run a pin through the top dot on each wedge and secure the pin. Do the same for the bottom dot.
3. Machine stitch between the pinned dots; backstitch to secure at both ends. (As with hand piecing, stitching between these points keeps the curved-edge seam allowance free for appliqué.)

 You may pair the wedges and chain-piece them as long as you remember to stitch only between the pinned dots.

Mariner's Compass

More than one quilter has uttered the words "Shiver me timbers!" (or something close to that) when attempting her first Mariner's Compass block. Truthfully, it will take more effort than the Grandmother's Fan, but it's worth it. Besides, you can do it. I have faith in you.

Let's look at what we know about this block:
- Most of the pieces have bias edges.
- The pieces to be joined are not identical shapes.

I'll say it one more time—bias edges stretch. The rays of the Mariner's Compass are thinner, so be extra careful with them. This warning applies both to hand and machine piecers.

If the pieces are not the same shape, how will we line them up for stitching? Let's address that question first. Hand piecers, you're up.

Hand Piecers

As a hand piecer, you have the advantage once again. When you hand piece, you match the pencil-line intersection points and begin and end your stitching at those points. You will do the same when hand piecing the Mariner's Compass. With equal-sized wedges, as in a Grandmother's Fan block, edges will align. Now, because the Mariner's Compass shapes are asymmetrical, the edges will not align.

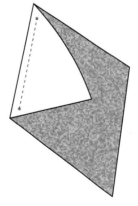

Asymmetrical shapes

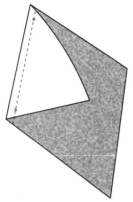

Machine Piecers

Prepare the templates for the Mariner's Compass (except the circle) just as you did for wedges. Match the dots and pin the pieces together. This time, however, you stitch through the points, not between them.

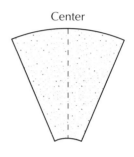

Stitch through points.

The machine piecers have been the "worker bees," busily learning new techniques. Well, hand piecers, it's time for you to get into the act.

You can make "Illusion" (page 37) using the machine technique below. Come on—this is for everybody.

Pieced Strips

Have you ever received praise for a dish you shared at a potluck that gave the appearance of taking a lot of time to prepare, when in fact it took very little? In one situation or another, most of us have enjoyed that feeling. In quiltmaking, pieced strips give us the same satisfaction.

1. Begin with a wedge template. Draw a line dividing the wedge equally through its center. Template C on page 57 provides this line. You will also need 2 strips of fabric. For "Illusion," cut the strips 2½" wide. If you are making your own strip-pieced wedges, see the Down the Road box on page 22 to determine the strip width.

Center

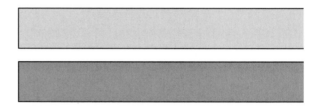

2. Join the strips by machine to make a strip set. Press the seam allowances toward the darker fabric.
3. Place the strip set wrong side up on your sandpaper board.
4. Align the center line of the template with the stitching line of the strip set.

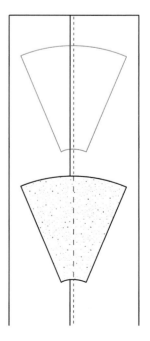

5. Trace around the template with a pencil.

6. If you used the hand-piecing template, cut ¼" from the pencil line for your seam allowances. If you used the machine-piecing template, cut on the line with scissors.

7. Continue to piece by hand or machine.

Be sure to leave a space between the wedges you trace. If you use the hand-piecing template, leave ¾" to 1". If you use the machine-piecing template, leave ½".

Look at the wedge from the right side. It already looks as though you spent more time on it than you did.

What do you think, hand piecers, are you willing to give it a go? If you are not convinced, you can still hand piece this wedge. Follow step 1 below to make a half-template. Repeat steps 2–4 for each wedge.

1. Trace only half of the hand-piecing template, including the center line.

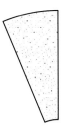

Half template

2. Trace the template once onto the first fabric. Cut ¼" from the line to add the seam allowances. Reverse the template and trace it again, this time on the second fabric. Cut ¼" from the line to add the seam allowances.

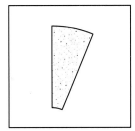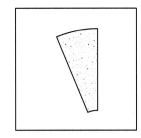

Template reversed

3. Place the fabric pieces right sides together and stitch the center seam.

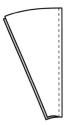

4. Press the seam allowances toward the darker fabric.

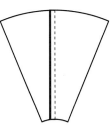

If you decide to make your own strip-pieced wedges, how wide must you cut your strips?

1. Measure the template from the center line through the widest part to the edge of the template. Let's say the measurement is 1¾".

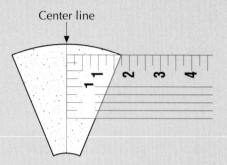

Center line

Hand-piecing template

2. If your template does not include seam allowances, add 1". If your template does include seam allowances, add ½". In this example, add 1" to the template measurement of 1¾" for a total of 2¾".

3. Cut each strip the width you just determined, 2¾" in this example, across the width of the fabric. You may not be able to cut the required number of wedges from just one strip set. If that's the case, you will need to cut and piece additional strips.

Since that went so well, let me show you another simple machine technique.

Easy Pointed Edges

Turn to Template D on page 63. This template looks strange, but you'll love what you can do with it. Make the template, trace it once onto a piece of fabric, and cut on the pencil line. Ready?

1. With right sides together, fold the wide, squared end in half and pin to hold.

2. Stitch from the outer edges toward the fold, using a ¼"-wide seam allowance; backstitch to secure. Trim the point at the fold to reduce bulk.

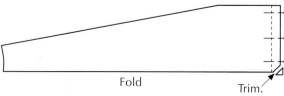

Fold

Trim.

3. Before you turn the wedge right side out, lightly finger-press the fold. Turn the point right side out and center the seam line on the crease. Press the point. This pointed edge is now prepared for appliqué.

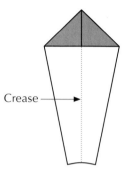

Crease

Mitered-Corner Borders

The "Grandmother's Fan Pillow" (page 35) features mitered-corner borders. With this border, you join border strips at a 45° angle. Admittedly, it takes more time to create a mitered-corner border than a straight-cut border, but it adds a special look to a project. Like anything you do for the first time, it involves a little effort. Each corner after the first one goes more quickly. Be patient with yourself.

These instructions use the measurements for the pillow on page 42. Working through the directions once will complete one corner. Repeat steps 5–7 to finish the remaining corners.

1. Fold a 3¼" x 17" border strip, wrong sides together, to find the midpoint; mark with a pin. Half of the finished pillow block measures 5", so on the edge with the pin, measure and mark a point 5" from the midpoint to the right and to the left.

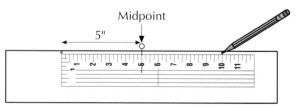

Midpoint

5"

Border strip

2. The unfinished block measurement is 10½" x 10½". Use a pin to mark the midpoint of one edge of the block. (It should be 5¼" from each end.) Right sides together, match the midpoints of the border strip and the block. The pencil marks added to the strip in step 1 should be ¼" from each end of the block. Pin the strip to the block. Sew the strip to the block between the marks, using a ¼"-wide seam allowance; backstitch to begin and end the stitching. Press the border away from the block.

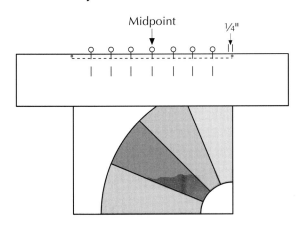

3. Repeat steps 1 and 2 for the remaining sides. Make sure your stitching lines do not cross.

 The border ends must be free beyond the marked points, or you will not be able to complete an accurate miter.

4. With the pillow top right side up, arrange the border strips so one end of each strip overlaps the next as shown.

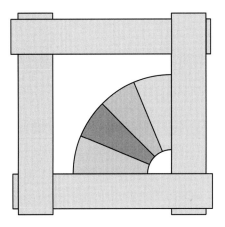

5. Flip the bottom border up and pin to hold it temporarily. Lift the right end of the bottom border and turn it up, creating a diagonal fold. Make sure the edges of the folded border and the outside edge of the right border are aligned. Press with a dry iron to crease.

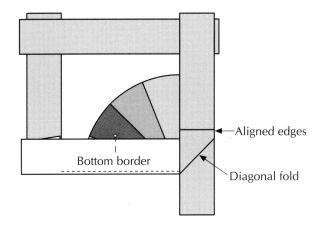

Remove the pin and return the border to the right side.

6. Fold the bottom border over until it is aligned with the edge of the right border. Pin at the crease.

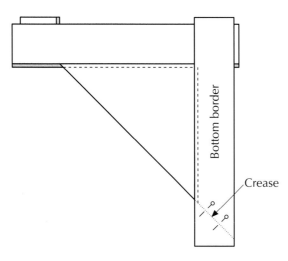

7. Sew on the creased line, beginning at the outside edge. Stop stitching just shy of the border seam line; backstitch to secure. Be sure to keep the inside border seam allowances free of the stitching. Trim the strips ¼" from the mitered stitching. Press the seam allowances to one side.

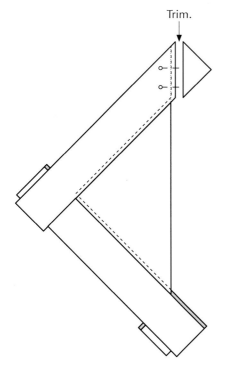

Hand Appliqué Techniques

You need to use appliqué in these projects, so arm yourself with your favorite method and the necessary supplies. If you're new to appliqué, get a copy of *Basic Quiltmaking Techniques for Hand Appliqué* to learn the basics.

Edges, Edges Everywhere

When you buy a new car, do you relish selecting the options? Maybe you look forward to the day you will own your own home and decorate it in a style that expresses who you are. If so, you will love this section.

As you have discovered, Mariner's Compass designs can take on a variety of appearances, yet all are based on the divided-circle technique. On the other hand, Fans and Dresden Plate blocks, also based on the divided-circle technique, are more instantly recognizable. Other than the number of wedges they contain, their general appearance is pretty much the same. Our opportunity to stylize these designs lies in their edges.

Treatment 1: The Smooth Edge

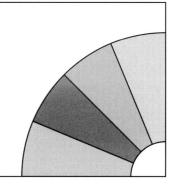

Smooth edge

You may also hear this edge referred to as a "plain" edge. It's the no-frills variety, consisting of an arc from the original circle. You may see smooth edges on Fan blocks and Dresden Plate blocks. Even though this edge is plain, you do have options.

Option A: The Basic Smooth Edge

To create this edge, simply prepare the edge and appliqué.

Option B: Lace-Trimmed Smooth Edge

1. With right sides together, place the raw edge of the lace within the seam allowance.
2. Attach the lace by stitching just shy of the ¼" seam-allowance line.
3. Fold the seam allowance under to reveal the lace-trimmed edge. The edge is now ready for appliqué.

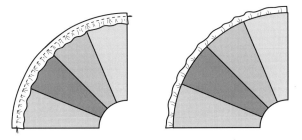

Treatments 2–4 embellish the smooth edge of Treatment 1.

Treatment 2: The Rounded Edge

Rounded edge

The rounded, or scalloped, edge gives your Fan or Dresden Plate a soft appearance.

Treatment 3: The Pointed Edge

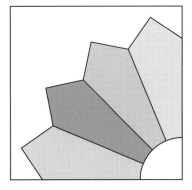

Pointed edge

The pointed edge, also known as the fancy point, gives the wedge of your Fan or Dresden Plate a crisp, tailored look. Refer to "Easy Pointed Edges" (page 22) and Template D (page 63) for a simple way to make these wedges.

Treatment 4: The Diagonal Edge

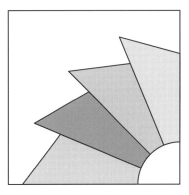

Diagonal edge

Another pointed-edge treatment provides a different look. None of the projects in this book use a diagonal edge, but I thought you might like to see it.

Inside Edges

Thought you were done with edges, didn't you? Well, you have another edge to take into consideration—the "inside edge." The small inside edge has options too.

Treatment 1

It's simple: using your method of appliqué, turn under the seam allowance and stitch.

Treatment 2

Instead of turning under the inside edges of the wedges, you can appliqué a circle to cover the raw edges at the seam line. The diameter of the cut circle must equal the distance between the finished lines of the wedges, plus the seam allowances. For example, if the distance between the finished lines of the wedges is 2", the circle must be cut 2½" in diameter.

Remember: With this treatment, it's not necessary to appliqué the inside edges of the wedges because the circle covers the raw edges.

Detail

 The fabric used for the appliquéd circle must be dark enough that none of the wedge colors shows through.

I hope this discussion hasn't made you edgy. (Sorry, I couldn't resist.) Think of the edges as "makeovers" for Fans and Dresden Plate blocks. We can all use a new look once in a while.

Positioning the Patchwork on the Background Fabric

You have selected your edge option and prepared accordingly for your method of appliqué. Now you are ready to position the patchwork on the background.

Divided-circle designs are based on circles—you know that. The shape of the patchwork to be appliquéd can be a quarter-circle (fan), a half-circle (half-fan), or a full circle (Dresden Plate). Positioning the patchwork on the background is not difficult. Follow these simple steps:

1. Determine the center of your patchwork. You need 1 line to find the center of a fan or a half-fan, and 2 lines to find the center of a Dresden Plate. Note that the center lines of your patchwork coincide with the seam lines between the wedges. Use the seam lines for easy matching in step 3.

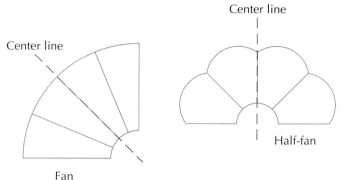

Fan

Half-fan

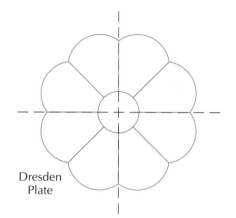

Dresden Plate

2. Determine the center of the background fabric by folding it in one of the ways shown below and on the following page; gently finger-press the fold to crease. Where there are two broken lines, fold in one direction first and finger-press. Open the background piece and fold it in the other direction; finger-press. For the on-point square, use only the vertical broken line to find the center for the fan.

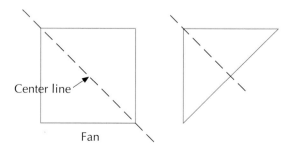

Center line

Fan

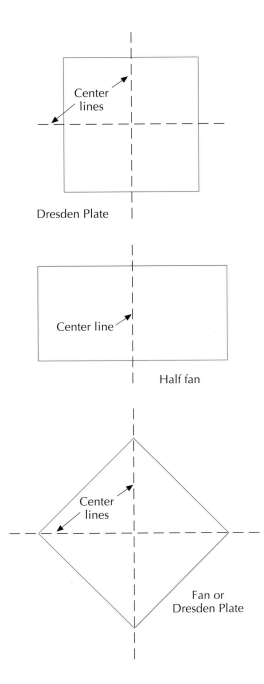

Dresden Plate

Half fan

Fan or
Dresden Plate

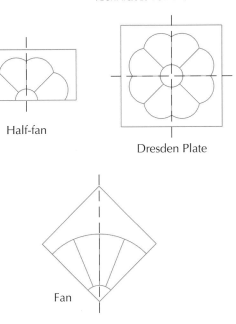

Half-fan

Dresden Plate

Fan

4. Pin the inner edges first, starting at the center point, then the outer edges. Add more pins as needed.

Thread Choice

Appliqué instructions usually direct you to match your thread to the color of your fabric. Usually, I do. However, when I appliqué a Dresden Plate, the wedges of the patchwork may be different colors. In this situation, I use a thread that blends nicely with both the background fabric and the wedge fabrics. Sometimes a neutral color like gray or tan works. My advice is to appliqué scraps of the wedge fabrics to a scrap of the background fabric. This test will also give you the opportunity to improve your appliqué stitch.

Stitching In-Side-Out

I had such fun coming up with that heading. Simply put, appliqué the smaller, inner edge of the patchwork first. Then appliqué the outside edge.

Even though you pin the patchwork in place, it can creep. Beginning at the inner edge helps to anchor the patchwork.

Stitching Out-Side-In

Appliqué involves turning under the edge of one piece and applying it to another. The Mariner's Compass gives us reason to rethink our approach to the appliqué portion of this divided circle.

3. Match the center of the patchwork with the creased line or lines of the background. The straight sides of fans and half-fans should be even with the sides of the background piece. Dresden Plates should match both the vertical and the horizontal lines.

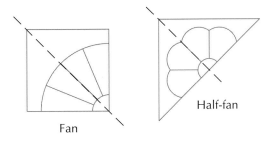

Fan

Half-fan

The Mariner's Compass block is a circle with lots of pieces. Some of those pieces come to a point at the outer edge of the circle. The outer edge of the circle is, in fact, a bias edge. (You know all about that, don't you?) If you turn under the edge of the circle to appliqué it, the points may lose their sharpness, and you will probably have a stretching problem.

The solution to this dilemma lies in reversing the roles of the background fabric and the patchwork. When you consider the Mariner's Compass circle as the *background* and appliqué the outside pieces of the block to it, you have a more manageable situation. This simple technique can add years to your life.

Once you have pieced your compass in quarters, you are ready to appliqué the outside pieces. In the example shown below, the background piece is Template L (page 77). Note that Template L has a dot indicating the center of the curved edge. Make a mark at this point on the seam line of the background piece.

The following steps complete one-quarter of the Mariner's Compass circle.

1. Using your method of appliqué, prepare the curved edge of the piece cut from Template L.
2. Place a pin at the center of the curved edge, at the point you marked.
3. Place a pin at the center of the compass quarter.

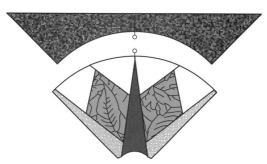

4. Overlap the curved edge of Piece L to meet the seam line of the compass quarter. Match the centers and pin. Match the outside edges and pin.

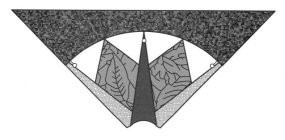

5. Make sure all edges of the curved piece meet the seam line of the compass quarter. Add more pins as needed.
6. Appliqué the curved edge of the background piece to the compass quarter.

Trimming the Background Fabric

You probably know how to trim your background fabric, but if you forgot to trim and end up quilting through all those layers, you'll never forgive me.

Turn the block over and trim the background fabric ¼" or so from the appliqué stitching line. You will also want to trim the extra layer on the wedges if you used the Easy Pointed Edges technique (page 22). The broken line in the illustration shows you where to trim.

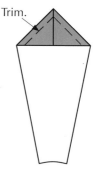

Trim.

A word of caution: please be very careful any time you trim. You will be heartbroken if, when trimming, you accidentally snip the right side of the design.

Go and digest all of this over a cup of tea. See you in a bit.

Drawing Divided-Circle Designs

Some of you are no doubt excited at the prospect of knowing how to draw divided-circle designs. It's a challenge, and you like challenges. Others will be shy and think, "I'm not ready for that." In either case, it's okay. This information will be presented as a Down the Road box, and you know what that means. So, if you are up for it, proceed. If you are not ready yet, take a peek after you complete a project or two.

This information may have a familiar ring because the concept is described in "Introduction to the Divided Circle" (page 11). This Down the Road box provides you with the instructions you need to draw your own divided circles. Remember the new tools at the beginning of the book? Well, now is your chance to use them. Gather your compass, drawing ruler, mechanical pencil, and graph paper. Ready, set, draw.

Dividing a Circle Equally
Exercise 1

1. Draw a square. Draw diagonal lines through the square in both directions. Where the 2 lines cross is the center point of the square.

2. Place the point of the compass exactly on the center point and draw a circle inside the square. Leave room between the circle's edge and the edge of the square. Remember: The diameter of the circle is twice the size of the compass setting. For example, a 2" compass setting will produce a circle that is 4" in diameter.

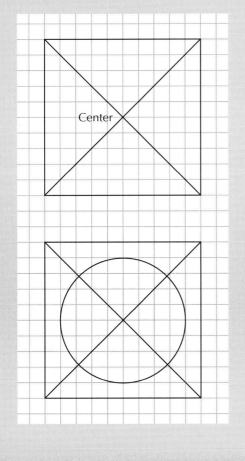

3. Draw vertical and horizontal lines through the center point to divide the square (and circle) in half both ways. The circle now has 8 equal sections.

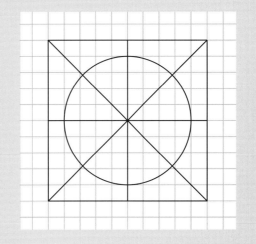

4. To further divide the circle, put the point of the compass on the top intersection point of the vertical dividing line and the circle. With the compass setting at about the distance to the diagonal dividing line, draw an arc above the circle between the 2 dividing lines. Keeping the same compass setting, put the point of the compass on the intersection of the diagonal dividing line and the circle. Draw a second arc, crossing the first arc.

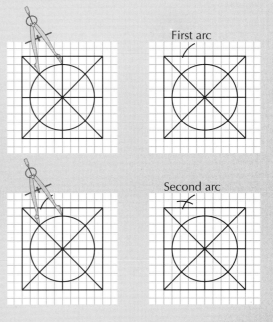

First arc

Second arc

Note: If the paper on which you are drawing is small or the square you have drawn is near the edge of the paper, the pencil may reach beyond the paper's edge when you try to draw the arcs. Should this happen, draw a new, smaller circle using the same center point. Draw the arcs using that circle.

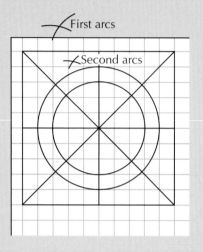

5. Draw a line connecting the center point of the circle and the intersection point of the crossed arcs. Notice the line you just drew equally divides 2 of the circle's 8 wedges.

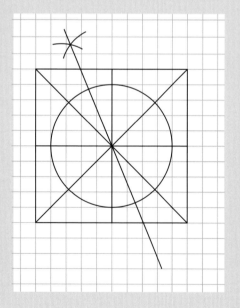

6. Repeat steps 4 and 5 to divide the other wedges. Now the circle is divided into 16 equal sections.

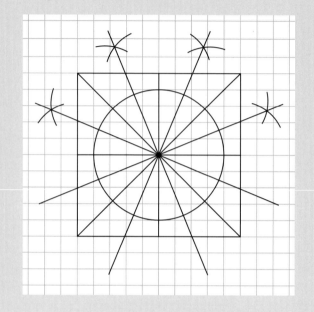

7. To make a smaller circle in the center, reduce the compass setting. Put the point of the compass on the center point you used for the original circle. Draw the smaller circle.

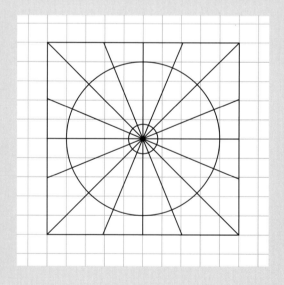

If you want to further divide the circle, repeat the steps.

Quarter Circle

One of the benefits of knowing how to draw a divided circle is that you can create a circle of any size and make the templates you need from your drawing. Because each wedge is equal, you can make your template by tracing a single wedge. For a block like Dresden Plate, you need only draw a quarter of a circle. For example, if you want a Dresden Plate for an 8" block, draw a 4" square and a quarter of the Dresden Plate design. If you want to appliqué the center circle on the Dresden Plate, you'll need to draw the entire center circle to make your template.

Drawing Edges on the Wedges
Exercise 2
Rounded Edge

To draw a rounded edge:

Place a small circular object on the end of the wedge. Make sure the object intersects both sides of the wedge. Trace around the object.

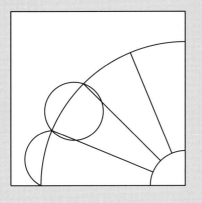

Pointed Edge

To draw a pointed edge:

1. Add a second arc beyond the original arc.
2. Draw the center line of the wedge. See Exercise 1, steps 4 and 5 on pages 29 and 30 to draw the center line.
3. Draw a line to connect one side of the wedge with the center line where it intersects the second arc.
4. Repeat on the other side of the wedge.

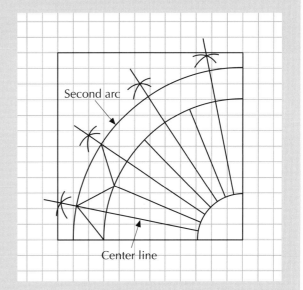

Second arc

Center line

If you are wondering what to use for a circular object, look in your kitchen. For the projects in this book I used two drinking glasses, a custard cup, and a votive container.

Diagonal Edge

To draw a diagonal edge:

1. Add a second arc beyond the original arc.
2. Extend the dividing lines to intersect the new arc.
3. Draw a diagonal line to connect the sides of the wedges as shown.

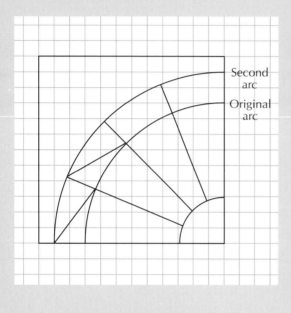

Second arc
Original arc

Drawing a Mariner's Compass

Don't let this block intimidate you. The very fact that it is a divided circle should remind you that you are simply adding to what you have learned.

Begin with steps 1–3 from Exercise 1. Your paper must accommodate a 7" square. For step 1, draw the square 7" x 7". This is not a magic number; it simply allows you to easily see what you are drawing. For step 2, draw a circle that is 6" in diameter (3" compass setting). Once you have completed step 3, your divided circle will have eight sections. Do step 7 from Exercise 1, making the circle 1" in diameter (½" compass setting). You are ready to proceed.

Can you see where to add the lines on your drawing to create the simple Mariner's Compass block in the illustration below? The solid lines are the first set of connecting lines to add. The broken lines are the second set of connecting lines to add. Continue with the next step.

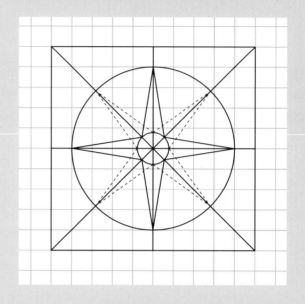

On your drawing, continue with steps 4–6 from Exercise 1 to create a circle with 16 divisions. With the point of the compass on the center point, draw another circle between the center circle and the outside circle. Make this circle 4" in diameter (2" compass setting).

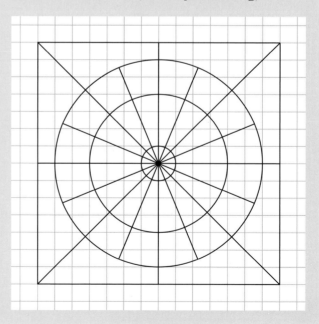

The next steps add connecting lines to your framework.

1. Draw a line to connect the vertical dividing line to the diagonal dividing line where they intersect, respectively, the outer and center circles. Repeat on the other side of the vertical dividing line. You have just made a ray.

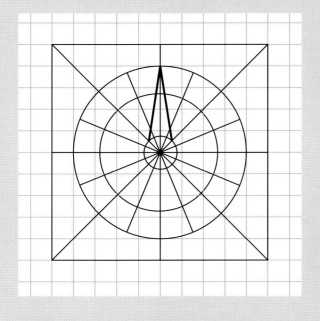

2. Repeat step 1 until your drawing looks like the illustration below.

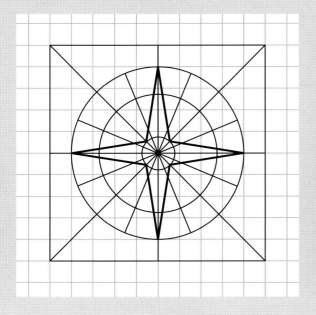

3. To create the next ray, draw a line to connect 2 adjacent diagonal lines where they intersect the outer and center circles, but stop your line when it meets the first ray you drew. (In the illustration below, the broken line indicates where the line would have been drawn if it had not stopped at the edge of the first ray.) Complete the ray by repeating this step on the other side of the diagonal dividing line.

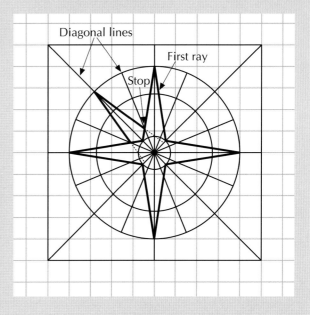

4. Repeat step 3 until your drawing looks like the illustration below.

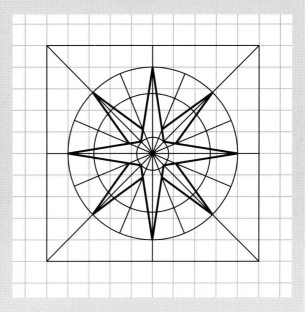

5. You are doing great! There are now only 8 dividing lines intersecting the outer circle that are unconnected. Draw a line to connect one of these intersection points with the middle circle where it meets a ray. Repeat on the other side of the dividing line. The addition of these lines creates a diamond shape.

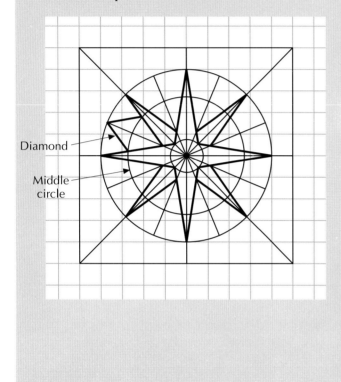

Diamond

Middle circle

6. Repeat step 5 until your drawing looks like the illustration below.

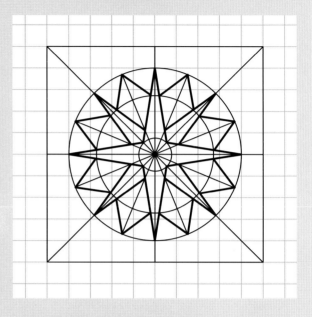

You did it—Bravo! Your drawing should resemble the Mariner's Compass block in the "Midnight Mariner" project (page 70). If you would like to try drawing a different Mariner's Compass, turn to the Down the Road box at the end of "Introduction to the Divided Circle" (page 13) for other design options.

You are now prepared to draw the divided circle of your dreams. Have fun doing it.

Gallery

Grandmother's Fan Pillow *by Sherry Reis, 1997, Worthington, Ohio, 15½ " x 15½ ". When made with a soft color scheme, this old-fashioned Fan block takes on a romantic flavor. Brighter, bolder fabrics would give a more contemporary look. This is a perfect project for anyone new to the divided-circle technique.*

Yuletide Table Runner by Sherry Reis, 1997, Worthington, Ohio, 12" x 36". A checked Christmas print inspired this table runner's holiday theme. Pick fabrics to complement your decor for everyday use. With only three blocks, it's a great beginner project.

Illusion *by Sherry Reis, 1997, Worthington, Ohio, 28" x 28".*
You create each two-toned wedge quickly using machine-pieced
strips. Light-, medium-, and dark-value background fabrics
give this quilt a dimensional, layered look.
The quilting emphasizes the illusion.

Oriental Fans *by Sherry Reis, 1997, Worthington, Ohio,*
30" x 30". Selecting fabrics for a quilt is easy if you start with a
multicolored fabric like the vibrant Oriental print used here and
then "pull" colors from it. The light background plays up the
bright hues of the fans, while the dark inner border and binding
give the appearance of a double frame. A simple machine
technique makes creating the fan points easy.

Delightful Dresdens *by Sherry Reis, 1998, Worthington, Ohio,*
28" x 28". A dramatic blue-and-white setting showcases striking
Dresden Plate blocks. Grid and straight-line quilting accent the
Dresden Plates, while a cable and simple scallop decorate
the dark borders. Made of only four blocks,
this is a project you will enjoy.

Midnight Mariner *by Sherry Reis, 1998, Worthington, Ohio, 32" x 32". A spectacular medallion setting encircles a lone Mariner's Compass block in this impressive project. The block is relatively simple but should not be taken lightly. A little experience will prepare you for the challenge. The compass and star setting appear to float on the airy, "night sky" fabric. Both hand and machine quilting emphasize and texture the design.*

Divided-Circle Projects

When proposing this book, one of the first steps I took was designing the six projects you see on the following pages. They were created, in part, to put into practice what you have learned about divided circles. They were also created because we are, after all, quilters, and working with fabric is what we do. It's the fun stuff.

For each project in this chapter, you will find "Project Information at a Glance," a materials list, step-by-step piecing instructions, and icons for hand piecing and machine piecing. Follow the instructions for the method you prefer.

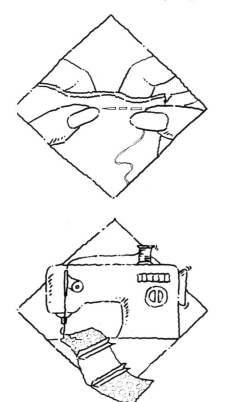

The steps will guide you through completion of the pillow and the table runner. The steps for the wall quilts end with the completed top and a quilting suggestion.

Now that you are quilting more, it is logical that your fabric stash has increased somewhat. (For some of you, "somewhat" is an understatement.) This increase is reflected in the number of fabrics the projects require. Don't let that throw you. Now is your chance to experiment with selecting fabrics.

I suggest that you begin the Block Assembly instructions for each project by laying out the fabric pieces for the entire block. The piecing sequence is more apparent when you do this step. The block assembly steps complete one block, but you may elect to work in assembly-line fashion. Do whatever works for you. If you are piecing by machine, look for the one-sided pressing arrows in the Quilt Top Assembly steps.

Get your supplies ready, and if you must, make a run to the quilt store for one more fabric. It is my wish that you have as much fun creating these projects as I did. Enjoy!

Grandmother's Fan Pillow

This project is the perfect place to start because it consists of only one block. The Grandmother's Fan is a simple Fan block with smooth-edge wedges. The second fabric listed in the Materials section gives you a design option. For straight-cut borders, use a multicolored fabric. For a stripe fabric, make mitered-corner borders, a more advanced technique. The pillow shown on page 35 has mitered-corner borders. Whether you piece by hand or machine, use your machine to construct the pillow after you complete the block.

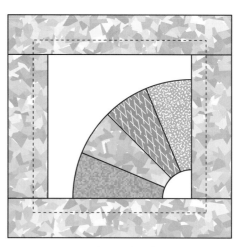

Straight-cut borders

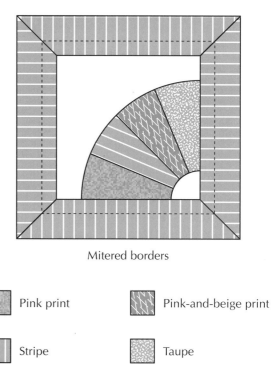

Mitered borders

Project Information at a Glance	
Finished Pillow Size:	15½" x 15½" (including the flange)
Name of Block:	Grandmother's Fan
Finished Block Size:	10" x 10"
Number of Blocks to Make:	1
Finished Border/ Flange Width:	2¾"
Outside Edge Treatment:	Smooth
Inside Edge Treatment:	Turned under

▨ Pink print		▨ Pink-and-beige print	
▤ Stripe		▦ Taupe	
▨ Multicolored		☐ Light tone-on-tone	

Materials: 42"-wide fabric

⅛ yd. pink print

⅝ yd. stripe or multicolored print (includes border/flange and pillow back)

⅛ yd. pink-and-beige print

⅛ yd. taupe

⅜ yd. light tone-on-tone print

12" x 12" square of muslin*

12" x 12" square of low-loft batting

12" x 12" pillow form

*This piece will be inside the pillow and will not be seen. Therefore, you may use muslin or any light-colored cotton fabric.

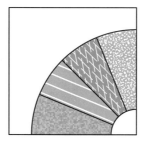

Grandmother's Fan
Make 1.

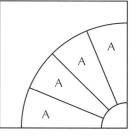

Letters identify template.

Cutting

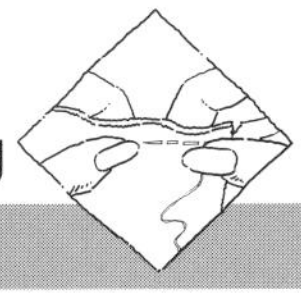

Setting Pieces

Fabric	No. of Pieces	Size to Mark	Size to Cut	Placement
Stripe*	4	2¾" wide	3¼" x 17"	borders/flange
Multicolor*	2	2¾" x 10"	3¼" x 10½"	side borders/flange
	2	2¾" x 15½"	3¼" x 16"	top and bottom borders/flange

Follow the cutting instructions for the fabric you have chosen.

Block Background

Fabric	No. of Pieces	Size to Mark	Size to Cut	Placement
Tone-on-tone	1	10" x 10"	10½" x 10½"	background

Cutting

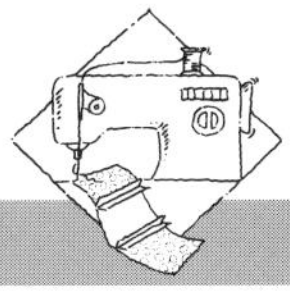

Setting Pieces

Fabric	No. of Pieces	Size to Rotary Cut	Placement
Stripe*	4	3¼" x 17"	borders/flange
Multicolor*	2	3¼" x 10½"	side borders/flange
	2	3¼" x 16"	top and bottom borders/flange

Follow the cutting instructions for the fabric you have chosen.

Block Background

Fabric	No. of Pieces	Size to Rotary Cut	Placement
Tone-on-tone	1	10½" x 10½"	background

Block Pieces to Mark and Cut

Make template A for hand piecing or machine piecing. If you use the hand-piecing template, remember to add ¼"-wide seam allowances when cutting the pieces. Cut the wedges carefully; with ⅛ yard, there is little room for error.

Fabric	No. of Pieces	Template
Pink	1	A
Stripe or multicolored	1	A
Pink-and-beige	1	A
Taupe	1	A

Block Assembly

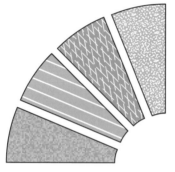

Lay out pieces.

The following example uses a striped fabric in the wedges.

1. Join a pink wedge (A) and a stripe wedge (A).

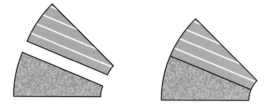

2. Join a pink-and-beige wedge (A) and a taupe wedge (A).

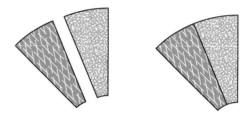

3. Join the units from step 1 and step 2.

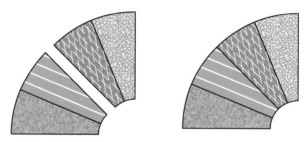

4. Prepare the edges for your method of appliqué.
5. Position the fan on the background square; pin to hold in place.
6. Appliqué the fan and trim the background fabric.

Pillow Assembly and Finishing

1. Layer the Fan block, batting square, and muslin square; baste. Quilt the block as desired by hand or machine, or follow the quilting suggestion below.

Quilting Suggestion

2. When you complete the quilting, machine or hand baste ⅛" from the outside edge; trim the batting and the backing fabric even with the edge of the Fan block.

3. If you are using a stripe print, turn to "Mitered-Corner Borders" (page 22) to add the stripe borders.

   If you are using a multicolored print, sew a 3¼" x 10½" border to each side of the Fan block. Sew a 3¼" x 16" border to the top and bottom of the Fan block.

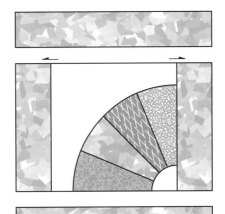

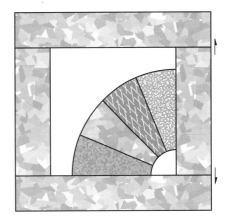

4. From the stripe or multicolored print, cut 2 rectangles, each 11" x 16". On one long side of each rectangle, turn under ½" twice and press. Machine stitch the edge.

5. With right sides together, place the long, unfinished edge of one rectangle even with the top edge of the pillow top and pin. Place the unfinished edge of the second rectangle even with the bottom edge of the pillow top and pin. Machine stitch around the edges using a ¼"-wide seam allowance; backstitch to secure. Trim the corners to reduce bulk.

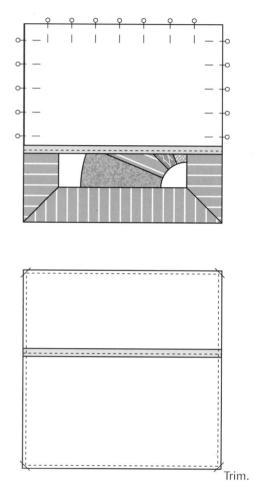

Trim.

6. Turn the pillow right side out and press the edges. Machine stitch the border 1" from the edge of the block (not the outer edge) to create the flange; backstitch to secure. Insert the pillow form.

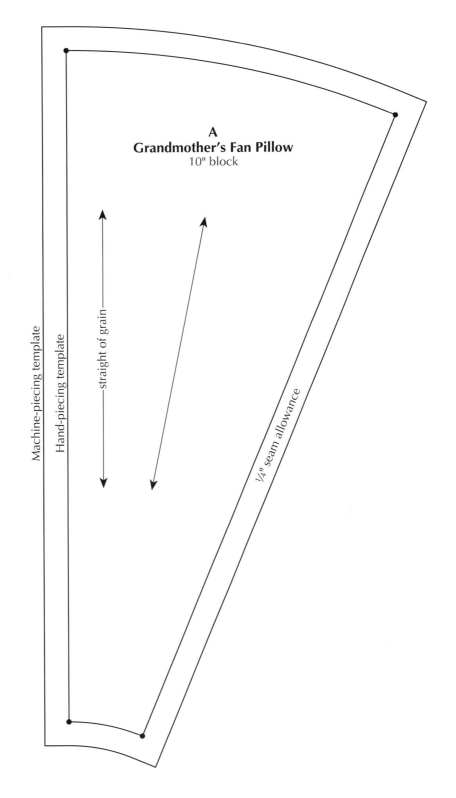

A
Grandmother's Fan Pillow
10" block

Machine-piecing template

Hand-piecing template

straight of grain

¼" seam allowance

Note: Finished-line points are for machine-piecing templates.
You can use either grain line when cutting piece A; refer to page 14.

Yuletide Table Runner

A checked Christmas tree fabric, which I found at my local quilt store, became the inspiration for this festive holiday table runner. Different colors will make it appropriate for any occasion. You'll have this three-block project completed in no time.

Project Information at a Glance	
Finished Runner Size:	12" x 36"
Name of Block:	Dresden Plate
Finished Block Size:	8½" x 8½"
Number of Blocks to Make:	3
Outside Edge Treatment:	Rounded
Inside Edge Treatment:	Turned under

Materials: 42"-wide fabric

½ yd. marbled green (includes binding)
¼ yd. red print
⅜ yd. white-on-white print
⅝ yd. Christmas tree check (includes backing)
16" x 40" piece of batting

 Marbled green   ☐ White-on-white print

 Red print   Christmas tree check

Dresden Plate
Make 3.

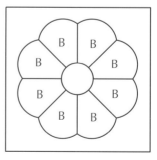

Letters identify template.

Cutting

Setting Pieces

Rotary cut the setting pieces for both hand and machine piecing. For hand piecing, mark the sewing lines ¼" from the edges.

Fabric	No. of Pieces	1st Rotary Cut	2nd Rotary Cut	Yield	Placement
Green	3	6⅞" x 6⅞"	◹	6	corner triangles
Red	3	6⅞" x 6⅞"	◹	6	corner triangles

◹ Cut the squares once diagonally.

Block Background

Fabric	No. of Pieces	Size to Mark	Size to Cut
White-on-white	3	8½" x 8½"	9" x 9"

Block Background

Fabric	No. of Pieces	Size to Rotary Cut
White-on-white	3	9" x 9"

Block Pieces to Mark and Cut

Make Template B for hand piecing or machine piecing. If you use the hand-piecing template, remember to add ¼"-wide seam allowances when cutting the pieces.

Fabric	No. of Pieces	Template
Green	12	B
Check	12	B

Block Assembly

Lay out pieces.

The directions that follow make one Dresden Plate block.

1. Join a green wedge (B) and a checked wedge (B).

Make 4.

2. Join 2 units from step 1. Repeat with another 2 units.

Make 2.

3. Join the 2 units from step 2.

4. Prepare the edges for your method of appliqué.
5. Center the patchwork on the background square; pin to hold in place.
6. Appliqué the patchwork and trim the background fabric.

Table Runner Assembly and Finishing

1. Fold each block in half, then in half again, and crease the folds at the edges to mark the midpoints. Fold each triangle in half along the long edge and gently crease the fold to mark the midpoint. The long edges of the triangles are on the bias, so handle them carefully.
2. Place the setting triangles around the block as shown in the photo on page 36. With right sides together, match the midpoint of one green triangle and the midpoint of one edge of the block. Pin. The triangle points will extend slightly beyond the edges of the block. Sew, using a ¼"-wide seam allowance. Press the seam allowances away from the block and trim the triangle points even with the unfinished edges. Repeat for the opposite green triangle.

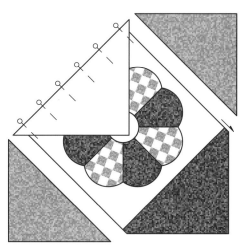

3. Pin and stitch the red triangles to the block to complete the block. Make the other 2 blocks.

5. Layer the runner top, batting, and backing; baste. Quilt as desired by hand or machine, or follow the quilting suggestion below.

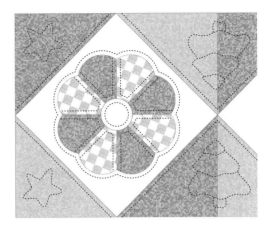

Quilting Suggestion

4. Join the 3 blocks.

6. Bind the edges.

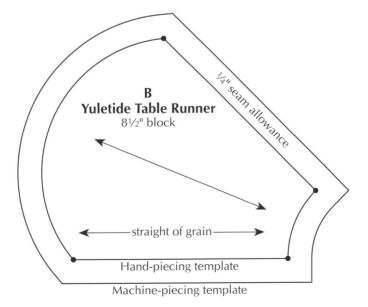

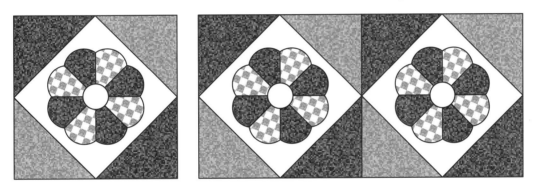

B
Yuletide Table Runner
8½" block

¼" seam allowance

straight of grain

Hand-piecing template

Machine-piecing template

Note: Finished-line points are for machine-piecing templates.
You can use either grain line when cutting piece B; refer to page 14.

Illusion

Have you ever been in the dressing room of a clothing store, where two mirrors reflect each other, creating so many images of you that you thought you'd gone into the next dimension? Okay, maybe just into a fun house. This quilt has a little of that sensation, but it's only an illusion. Look at the large circle in the center of the quilt. If you took all the other wedges and formed circles like the center one, you would have only three more! It looks like more, doesn't it? Go ahead—make this quilt and impress everyone you know.

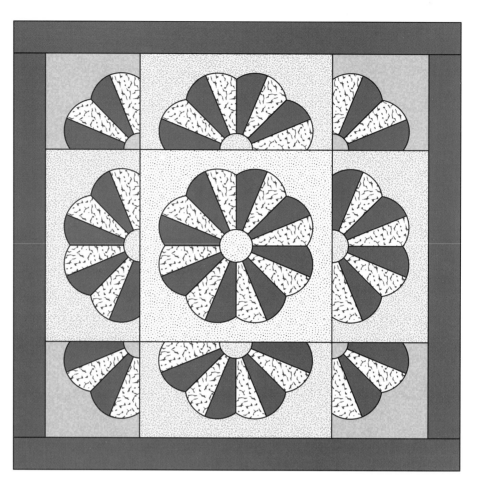

Project Information at a Glance

Finished Quilt Size:	28" x 28"
Name of Block:	Art Deco Fans
Finished Block Size:	6" x 6" (corner)
	6" x 12" (edge)
	12" x 12" (center)
Number of Blocks to Make:	4 (corner)
	4 (edge)
	1 (center)
Outside Edge Treatment:	Rounded
Inside Edge Treatment:	Turned under

Materials: 42"-wide fabric

1 yd. dark rust print (includes borders and binding)

1⅝ yds. leaf print (includes backing and 10" sleeve)

½ yd. light crackled print

½ yd. medium taupe print

¼ yd. medium-dark gray print

32" x 32" square of batting

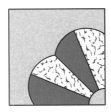

Art Deco Fans
Make 4.

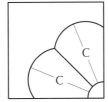

Letters identify
template.

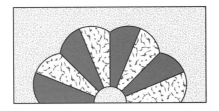

Make 4.

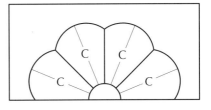

Make 1.

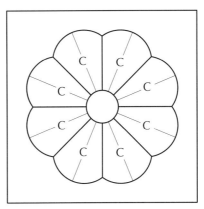

Rust print

Leaf print

Crackled print

Taupe print

Gray print

Cutting

Setting Pieces

Cut the border strips from selvage to selvage across the width of the fabric.

Fabric	No. of Pieces	Size to Mark	Size to Cut	Placement
Rust	2	2" x 24"	2½" x 24½"	side borders
	2	2" x 28"	2½" x 28½"	top and bottom borders

Block Background

Fabric	No. of Pieces	Size to Mark	Size to Cut	Placement
Crackled print	1	12" x 12"	12½" x 12½"	center background
Taupe	4	6" x 12"	6½" x 12½"	edge background
Gray	4	6" x 6"	6½" x 6½"	corner background

Cutting

Setting Pieces

Cut the border strips from selvage to selvage across the width of the fabric.

Fabric	No. of Pieces	Size to Rotary Cut	Placement
Rust	2	2½" x 24½"	side borders
	2	2½" x 28½"	top and bottom borders

Block Background

Fabric	No. of Pieces	Size to Rotary Cut	Placement
Crackled print	1	12½" x 12½"	center background
Taupe	4	6½" x 12½"	edge background
Gray	4	6½" x 6½"	corner background

Block Pieces to Mark and Cut

See "Pieced Strips" on page 20 for complete instructions.

Fabric	No. of Pieces	Size to Rotary Cut
Rust	4	2½" x width of fabric
Leaf print	4	2½" x width of fabric

Make Template C for hand piecing or machine piecing. If you use the hand-piecing template, remember to add ¼"-wide seam allowances when cutting the pieces.

Fabric	No. of Pieces	Template
Pieced strips	32	C

Block Assembly

Lay out pieces.

1. Join 2 wedges (Template C). This is Unit A. Set aside the units for the corner blocks.

Unit A
Make 4.

2. Make 2 of Unit A and join to make a half-circle. This is Unit B. Set aside the units for the edge blocks.

Unit B
Make 4.

3. Make 4 of Unit A and join to make a complete circle for the center block. This is Unit C.

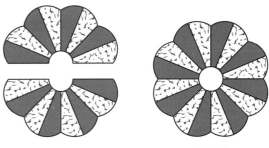

Unit C
Make 1.

4. Prepare the edges for your method of appliqué.
5. Position the patchwork units on the background pieces. Place each Unit A on a small square, each Unit B on a rectangle, and Unit C on the large square. Pin in place to hold.
6. Appliqué the patchwork and trim the background fabrics.

Quilt Top Assembly

1. Arrange the units as shown in the quilt plan.
2. Join the units to make 3 horizontal rows. Join the rows to complete the quilt center.

3. Add the side borders first, followed by the top and bottom borders.

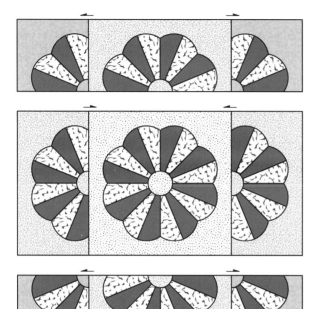

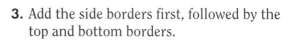

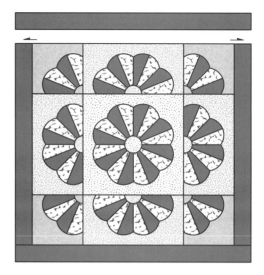

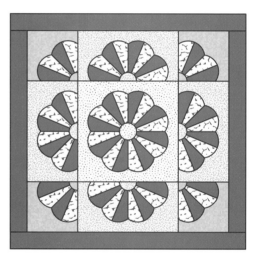

4. Layer the quilt top, batting, and backing; baste. Quilt as desired by hand or machine, or follow the quilting suggestion below.

5. Bind the edges.

Quilting Suggestion

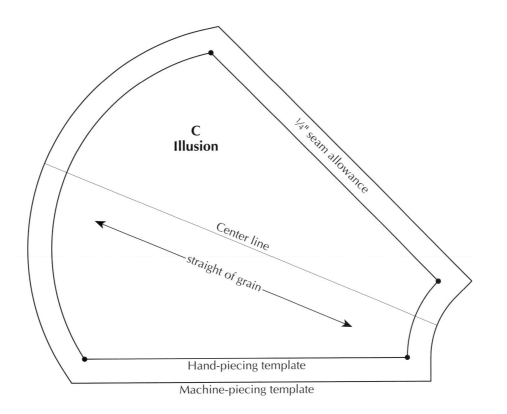

C
Illusion

¼" seam allowance

Center line

straight of grain

Hand-piecing template

Machine-piecing template

Note: Finished-line points are for machine-piecing templates.

Oriental Fans

Making choices is a snap for some people. For others, it can be stressful. If selecting fabrics makes you anxious, this project can help. When you pick a multicolored fabric, like the one used here, the other colors are already chosen for you. Aren't you the smart one for picking such a special fabric? Simply pull fabric colors found in the print.

The edge treatment on the fans in this quilt is pointed. Use the machine-piecing template and the lesson for "Easy Pointed Edges" (page 22), and you'll have them ready in a jiffy.

Project Information at a Glance	
Finished Quilt Size:	30" x 30"
Name of Block:	Mary's Fan
Finished Block Size:	8½" x 8½"
Number of Blocks to Make:	4
Outside Edge Treatment:	Pointed
Inside Edge Treatment:	Turned under

Materials: 42"-wide fabric

1⅝ yds. white print (includes backing and 10" sleeve)

⅛ yd. purple print

⅛ yd. green print

⅛ yd. lavender print

⅛ yd. red print

½ yd. black tone-on-tone print (includes inner border and binding)

¾ yd. multicolored print (includes outer border)

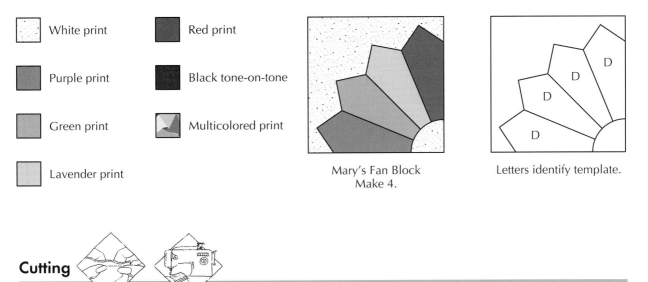

White print
Red print
Purple print
Black tone-on-tone
Green print
Multicolored print
Lavender print

Mary's Fan Block
Make 4.

Letters identify template.

Cutting

Setting Pieces

Rotary cut the setting pieces for both hand and machine piecing. For hand piecing, mark the sewing line ¼" from the edges. Cut the border strips from selvage to selvage across the width of the fabric.

Fabric	No. of Pieces	1st Rotary Cut	2nd Rotary Cut	Yield	Placement
Black	2	1½" x 24½"			side inner borders
	2	1½" x 26½"			top and bottom inner borders
Multicolored	2	2½" x 26½"			side outer borders
	2	2½" x 30½"			top and bottom outer borders
	1	9" x 9"			center square
	1	13¼" x 13¼"	⊠	4	side triangles
	2	6⅞" x 6⅞"	◻	4	corner triangles

⊠ Cut the squares twice diagonally. ◻ Cut the squares once diagonally.

Block Background

Fabric	No. of Pieces	Size to Mark	Size to Cut
White	4	8½" x 8½"	9" x 9"

Block Background

Fabric	No. of Pieces	Size to Rotary Cut
White	4	9" x 9"

Block Pieces to Mark and Cut

For machine piecing, make Template D (page 63) to use with the Easy Pointed Edges technique (page 22). For hand piecing, make a finished-size Template D. (You cannot use this template with the Easy Pointed Edges technique.) If you use the hand-piecing template, remember to add ¼"-wide seam allowances when cutting the pieces.

Fabric	No. of Pieces	Template
Purple	4	D
Green	4	D
Lavender	4	D
Red	4	D

Block Assembly

Lay out pieces.

The instructions below will make one Fan block.

1. Join a purple and a green wedge (D).

2. Join a lavender and a red wedge (D).

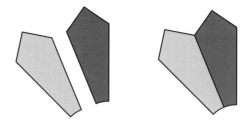

3. Join the units from step 1 and step 2.

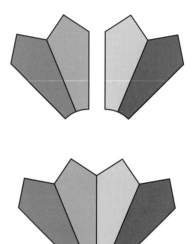

4. Prepare the edges for appliqué.
5. Position each fan on a background square and pin to hold in place.
6. Appliqué the fans and trim the background fabric. If you made the fans with Easy Pointed Edges, trim the points.

Quilt Top Assembly

1. Arrange the blocks and setting pieces in diagonal rows.

2. Join each corner section first, adding the side triangles, followed by the corner triangle. All joining edges of the triangles are on the bias, so pin them carefully before sewing.

    Join the blocks and corner triangles to make the center row. Join the corner sections and the center row.

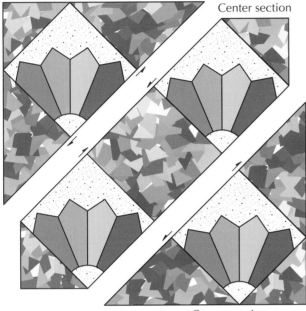

Corner section

Center section

Corner section

3. Add the inner borders to the sides of the quilt top, followed by the top and bottom inner borders.

4. Add the outer borders to the sides of the quilt top, followed by the top and bottom outer borders.

5. Layer the quilt top with batting and backing; baste. Quilt as desired by hand or machine, or follow the quilting suggestion below.

6. Bind the edges.

Quilting Suggestion

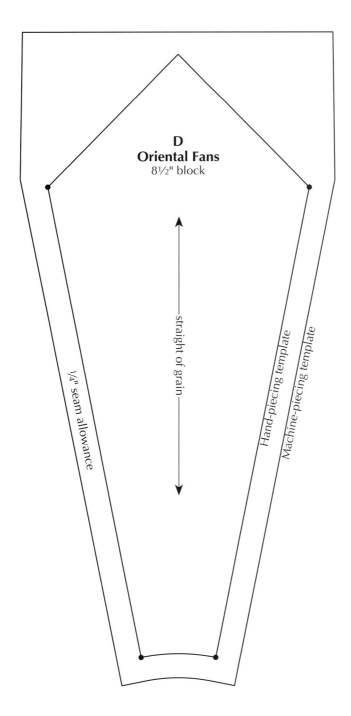

D
Oriental Fans
8½" block

straight of grain

¼" seam allowance

Hand-piecing template

Machine-piecing template

Note: Finished-line points are for machine-piecing templates.

Delightful Dresdens

Although it may not be obvious to you, Delightful Dresdens is a four-block quilt. You appliqué the center Dresden Plate after you join the blocks, creating a quilt that looks more complicated than it actually is. Choose fabrics in shades of one color, as in the quilt shown on page 39. A scrappy look would work just as well.

Project Information at a Glance	
Finished Quilt Size:	28" x 28"
Name of Block:	Dresden Plate (variation)
Finished Block Size:	12" x 12"
Number of Blocks to Make:	4
Outside Edge Treatment:	Rounded
Inside Edge Treatment:	Turned under

Materials: 42"-wide fabric

¾ yd. white-on-white print

¼ yd. dark blue floral

¼ yd. medium blue paisley

¼ yd. blue cracked ice

1½ yds. light blue floral (includes backing and 10" sleeve)

¾ yd. dark blue vine (includes border and binding)

White-on-white

Dark blue floral

Medium blue paisley

Blue cracked ice

Light blue floral

Dark blue vine

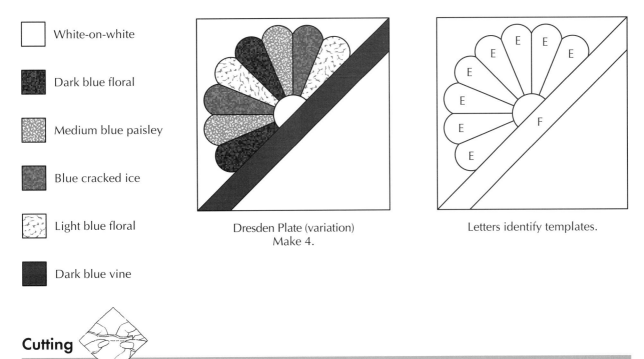

Dresden Plate (variation)
Make 4.

Letters identify templates.

Cutting

Setting Pieces

Cut the border strips from selvage to selvage across the width of the fabric.

Fabric	No. of Pieces	Size to Mark	Size to Cut	Placement
Dark blue vine	2	2" x 24"	2½" x 24½"	side borders
	2	2" x 28"	2½" x 28½"	top and bottom borders

Cutting

Setting Pieces

Cut the border strips from selvage to selvage across the width of the fabric.

Fabric	No. of Pieces	Size to Rotary Cut	Placement
Dark blue vine	2	2½" x 24½"	side borders
	2	2½" x 28½"	top and bottom borders

Block Background

Rotary cut the background pieces for both hand and
machine piecing. For hand piecing, mark sewing lines ¼" from the edges.

Fabric	No. of Pieces	1st Rotary Cut	2nd Rotary Cut	Yield	Placement
White-on-white	2	12⅞" x 12⅞"	◹	4	corner triangles
	2	10⅞" x 10⅞"	◹	4	inner triangles

◹ Cut the squares once diagonally.

Block Pieces to Mark and Cut

Make Template E and Template F for hand piecing or machine piecing. If you use the hand-piecing templates, remember to add ¼"-wide seam allowances when cutting the pieces.

Fabric	No. of Pieces	Template
Dark blue floral	12	E
Medium blue paisley	12	E
Blue cracked ice	12	E
Light blue floral	12	E
Dark blue vine	4	F

Block Assembly

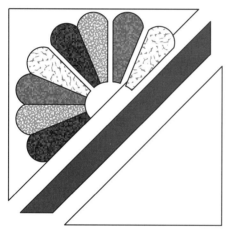

Lay out pieces.

The instructions below will make one block.

1. Join a blue floral wedge (E) and a blue paisley wedge (E). Join a blue ice wedge (E) and a light blue wedge (E).

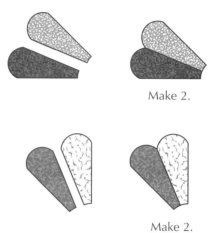

Make 2.

Make 2.

2. Join the units made in the previous step.

Make 2.

3. Join the units made in the previous step to make a half Dresden Plate.

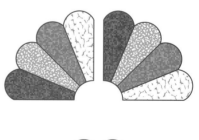

4. The long edge of the background triangle used in this step is on the bias, so be careful not to stretch it. Fold a small (10⅞") background triangle and one dark blue strip (F) in half and crease to mark the midpoints. With right sides together, match the midpoints of the triangle and the strip, and pin. Stitch, using a ¼"-wide seam allowance.

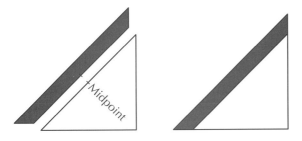

5. Prepare the edges for your method of appliqué.

6. Position the patchwork from step 3 on a large (12⅞") background triangle, being careful not to stretch the bias edge of the triangle. Pin the patchwork to the background triangle.

7. Appliqué the patchwork and trim the background fabric.

8. With right sides together, pin the unit from step 4 and the unit from step 7. Stitch, using a ¼"-wide seam allowance, to make 1 block. Repeat to make 3 additional blocks.

Center Dresden Plate

1. Follow steps 1–3 of "Block Assembly" to make a half Dresden Plate. Repeat to make an additional half Dresden Plate.

2. Join the units to make the center Dresden Plate.

3. Prepare the edges for your method of appliqué and set the patchwork aside.

Quilt Top Assembly

1. Arrange the blocks as shown. Join the top blocks. Join the bottom blocks. Join the top half and the bottom half.

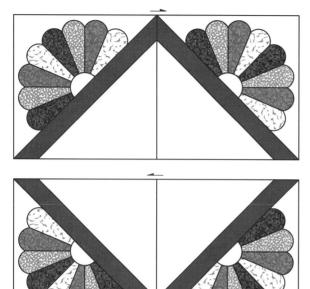

2. Position the Dresden Plate on the center of the quilt, using the seam lines as a guide. Pin the patchwork to hold it in place.

3. Appliqué the patchwork and trim the background fabric.

4. Add the side borders to the quilt top, followed by the top and bottom borders.

5. Layer the quilt top with batting and backing; baste. Quilt as desired, or follow the quilting suggestion below.

6. Bind the edges.

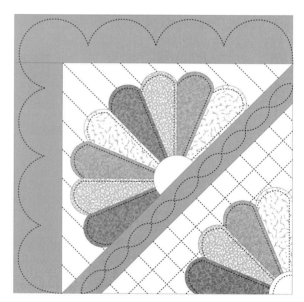

Quilting Suggestion

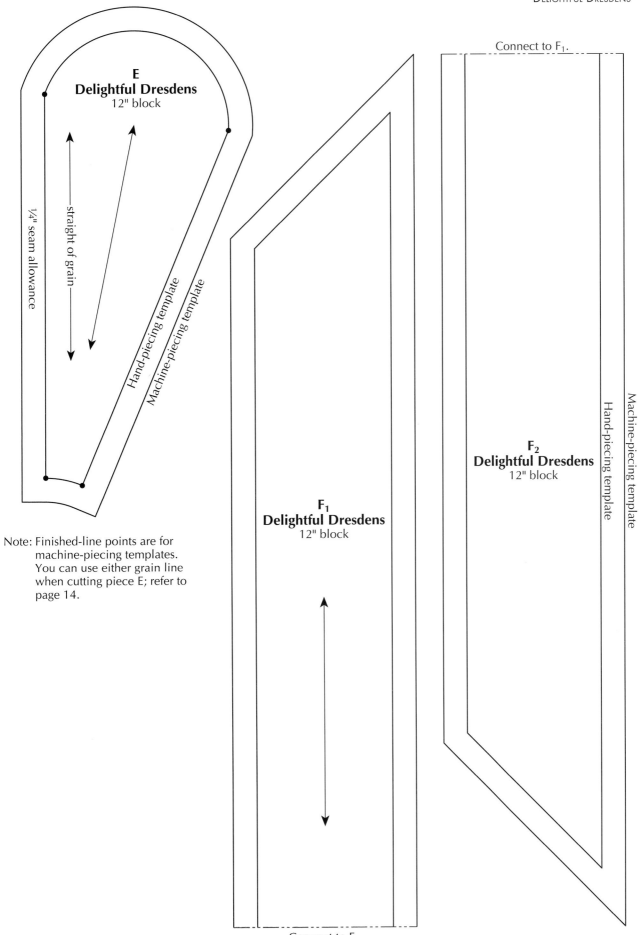

E
Delightful Dresdens
12" block

¼" seam allowance

straight of grain

Hand-piecing template

Machine-piecing template

Note: Finished-line points are for machine-piecing templates. You can use either grain line when cutting piece E; refer to page 14.

Connect to F₁.

F₂
Delightful Dresdens
12" block

Hand-piecing template

Machine-piecing template

F₁
Delightful Dresdens
12" block

Connect to F₂.

Midnight Mariner

Always dramatic, the Mariner's Compass block is a crowd pleaser. The experience you have gained from doing the earlier projects will give you the confidence to do this one-block quilt. Work through the steps carefully for a rewarding experience. Special appliqué instructions can be found in "Stitching Out-Side-In" on pages 27–28.

Project Information at a Glance

Finished Quilt Size:	32" x 32"
Name of Block:	Mariner's Compass
Finished Block Size:	14" x 14"
Number of Blocks To Make:	1
Inside Edge Treatment:	Covered with circle

Materials: 42"-wide fabric

¼ yd. light gray print

¼ yd. medium gray print

⅜ yd. red print

2¼ yds. black tone-on-tone (includes border, backing, binding, and 10" sleeve)

¾ yd. night-sky print

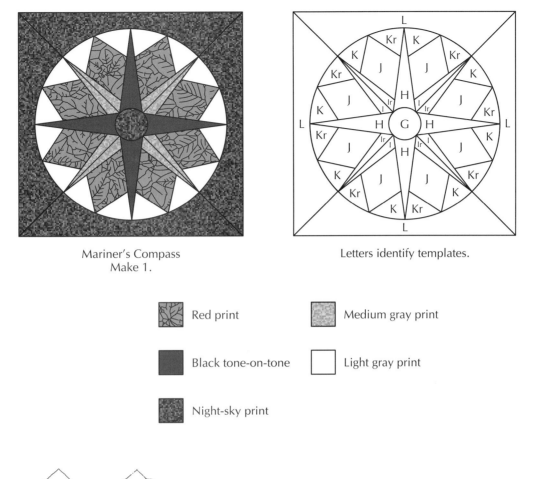

Mariner's Compass
Make 1.

Letters identify templates.

Red print

Medium gray print

Black tone-on-tone

Light gray print

Night-sky print

Cutting

Setting Pieces

Rotary cut the setting pieces for both hand and machine piecing. For hand piecing, mark the sewing line ¼" from the edges. Cut the border strips from selvage to selvage across the width of the fabric.

Fabric	No. of Pieces	1st Rotary Cut	2nd Rotary Cut	Yield	Placement
Red	2	8¼" x 8¼"	⊠	8	small setting triangles
Black	1	15¼" x 15¼"	⊠	4	large setting triangles
	2	2½" x 28½"			side borders
	2	2½" x 32½"			top and bottom borders
Night-sky	4	7½" x 7½"			corner squares
	2	8¼" x 8¼"	⊠	8	small setting triangles

⊠ Cut the squares twice diagonally.

Block Pieces to Mark and Cut		
Fabric	**No. of Pieces**	**Template**
Black	4	H
Medium gray	4	I
	4	I reversed
Red	8	J
Light gray	8	K
	8	K reversed
Night-sky	4	L
	1	G

Block Assembly

Lay out pieces.

The instructions below are for one-quarter of the compass. The "r" with a template letter indicates that the piece is reversed. Most edges are on the bias, so be extremely careful not to stretch the pieces. Pin carefully before sewing. See "Mariner's Compass" on pages 19–20 for piecing tips.

1. Join a light gray wedge (K) and a red diamond (J).

Make 2.

2. Join a light gray wedge (Kr) to each unit.

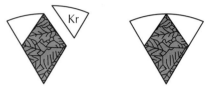

Make 2.

3. Join a medium gray ray (I) to the right edge of a unit.

4. Join a medium gray ray (Ir) to the left edge of a unit.

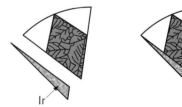

5. Join the unit made in step 3 to the right edge of a black ray (H).

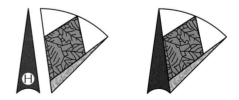

6. Join the unit made in step 4 to the left edge of the unit.

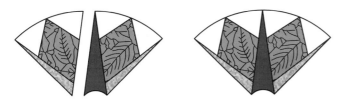

7. Referring to "Stitching Out-Side-In" on pages 27–28, prepare the edge of night-sky piece L and appliqué it to the compass quarter made in step 6. Make 3 more compass quarters.
8. Join 2 compass quarters to make one-half of the block. Join the other 2 quarters to make the second half of the block. Join the 2 halves.

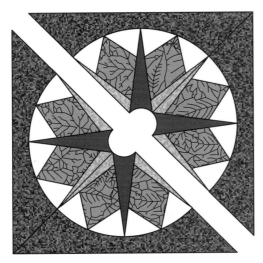

9. Prepare the edges and appliqué the circle (G) to the center of the block.

Setting Assembly

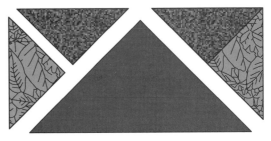

Lay out the pieces.

The directions that follow are for one setting unit. The triangle edges that you join are on the bias, so be careful not to stretch them. Pin carefully before joining.

1. Join a red triangle and a night-sky triangle.

2. Join a night-sky triangle and a red triangle.

3. Join the unit made in step 1 to the left edge of a large black setting triangle.

4. Join the unit made in step 2 to the right edge of the unit made in step 3.

Quilt Top Assembly

1. Arrange the corner setting squares, setting units, and Mariner's Compass block as shown. Join the units to make 3 rows. Join the rows to make the quilt center.

2. Add the side borders, followed by the top and bottom borders.

4. Layer the quilt top with batting and backing; baste. Quilt as desired by hand or machine, or follow the quilting suggestion below.

5. Bind the edges.

Quilting Suggestion

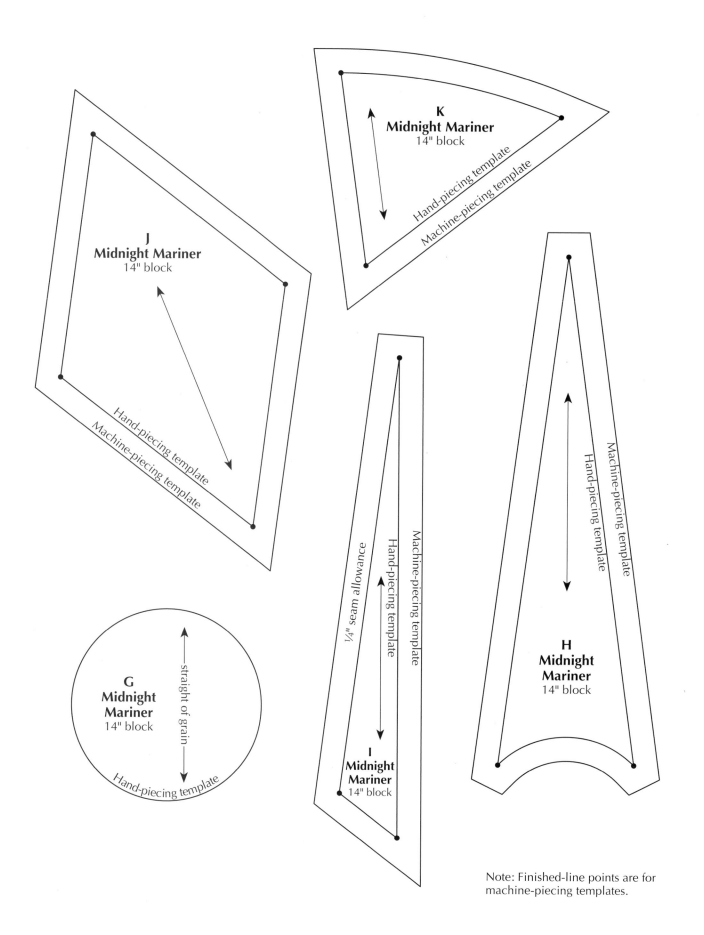

K
Midnight Mariner
14" block

Hand-piecing template
Machine-piecing template

J
Midnight Mariner
14" block

Hand-piecing template
Machine-piecing template

G
Midnight Mariner
14" block

straight of grain

Hand-piecing template

¼" seam allowance

Machine-piecing template

Hand-piecing template

I
Midnight Mariner
14" block

Machine-piecing template
Hand-piecing template

H
Midnight Mariner
14" block

Note: Finished-line points are for machine-piecing templates.

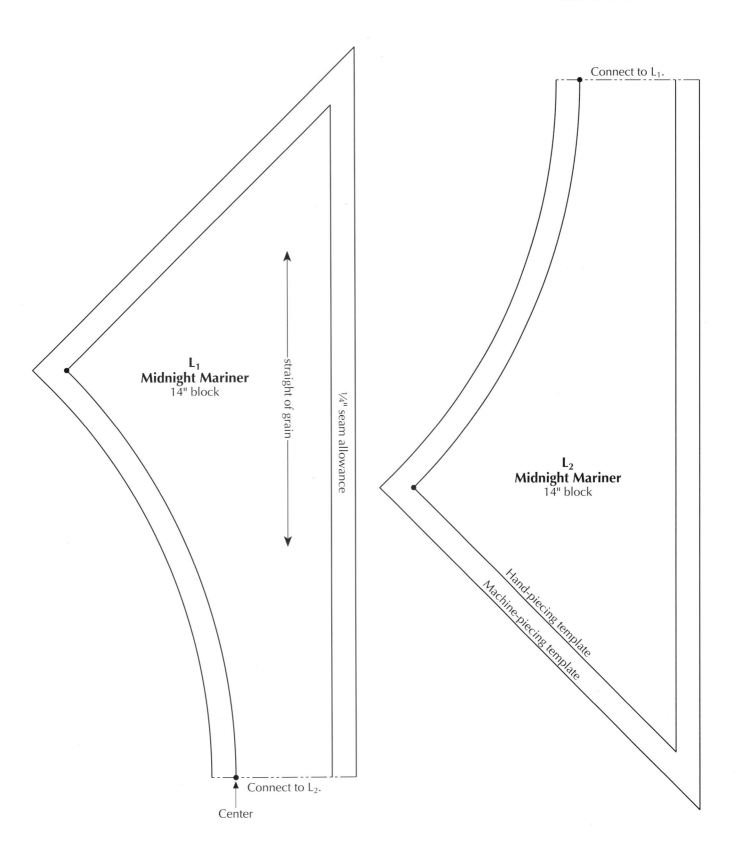

L₁
Midnight Mariner
14" block

straight of grain

¼" seam allowance

Connect to L₁.

Connect to L₂.

Center

L₂
Midnight Mariner
14" block

Hand-piecing template
Machine-piecing template

Note: Finished-line points are for machine-piecing templates.
On Template L, the center finished-line point is necessary
for both hand and machine piecing.

Happy Trails

Whenever you spend time doing something you truly love—like quilting—and doing that activity with people that are fun, energetic, and a joy to be with—like quilters—it's hard to part company.

Through this book, you and I have shared the experience of learning what divided circles are all about. I hope the experience was as worthwhile for you as it was for me.

Every one of us leads a busy life. Quite often, it is hard to find time "just for you," but make time. Make time to work on your projects, to give yourself the opportunity to learn more about this fine art of quiltmaking, and to share it all with the remarkable community of women and men known as quilters. Believe me, you won't regret the decision.

Well, not one to have ever liked good-byes, how about if I say, "Till we meet again."

Bibliography

Beyer, Jinny. *Patchwork Patterns*. McLean, Va.: EPM Publications, 1979.

Brackman, Barbara. *Encyclopedia of Pieced Quilt Patterns*. Paducah, Ky.: American Quilter's Society, 1993.

Dietrich, Mimi. *Basic Quiltmaking Techniques for Hand Appliqué*. Bothell, Wash.: That Patchwork Place, 1998.

Doak, Carol. *Quiltmaker's Guide: Basics & Beyond*. Paducah, Ky.: American Quilter's Society, 1992.

———. *Your First Quilt Book (or it should be!)*. Bothell, Wash.: That Patchwork Place, 1997.

Mathieson, Judy. *Mariner's Compass: An American Quilt Classic*. Lafayette, Calif.: C&T Publishing, 1987.

Meet the Author

Sherry Reis learned to quilt through an adult education class in 1979. What began as a hobby blossomed into a passion. Teaching, lecturing, and of course making quilts, fill most of her days.

Several of Sherry's quilts have appeared in quiltmaking books and have been featured in national publications. One of Sherry's creations graces the wall of a local hospital.

An active member of the quilting community, she belongs to several quilt guilds, where she enjoys the friendship and common bond of fellow quilters.

Worthington, Ohio, is home to Sherry and her family, who are certain she owns stock in a fabric company.

Books from Martingale & Company

Appliqué

Appliquilt® Your ABCs
Appliquilt® to Go
Baltimore Bouquets
Basic Quiltmaking Techniques for Hand Appliqué
Coxcomb Quilt
The Easy Art of Appliqué
Folk Art Animals
From a Quilter's Garden
Stars in the Garden
Sunbonnet Sue All Through the Year
Traditional Blocks Meet Appliqué
Welcome to the North Pole

Borders and Bindings

Borders by Design
The Border Workbook
A Fine Finish
Happy Endings
Interlacing Borders
Traditional Quilts with Painless Borders

Design Reference

All New! Copy Art for Quilters
Blockbender Quilts
Color: The Quilter's Guide
Design Essentials: The Quilter's Guide
Design Your Own Quilts
Fine Art Quilts
Freedom in Design
The Log Cabin Design Workbook
Mirror Manipulations
The Nature of Design
QuiltSkills
Sensational Settings
Surprising Designs from Traditional Quilt Blocks
Whimsies & Whynots

Foundation/Paper Piecing

Classic Quilts with Precise Foundation Piecing
Crazy but Pieceable
Easy Machine Paper Piecing
Easy Mix & Match Machine Paper Piecing
Easy Paper-Pieced Keepsake Quilts
Easy Paper-Pieced Miniatures
Easy Reversible Vests
Go Wild with Quilts
Go Wild with Quilts—Again!
A Quilter's Ark
Show Me How to Paper Piece

Hand and Machine Quilting/Stitching

Loving Stitches
Machine Needlelace and Other
  Embellishment Techniques
Machine Quilting Made Easy
Machine Quilting with Decorative Threads
Quilting Design Sourcebook
Quilting Makes the Quilt
Thread Magic
Threadplay with Libby Lehman

Home Decorating

Decorate with Quilts & Collections
The Home Decorator's Stamping Book
Living with Little Quilts
Make Room for Quilts
Soft Furnishings for Your Home
Welcome Home: Debbie Mumm

Miniature/Small Quilts

Beyond Charm Quilts
Celebrate! with Little Quilts
Easy Paper-Pieced Miniatures
Fun with Miniature Log Cabin Blocks
Little Quilts All Through the House
Lively Little Logs
Living with Little Quilts
Miniature Baltimore Album Quilts
No Big Deal
A Silk-Ribbon Album
Small Talk

Needle Arts/Ribbonry

Christmas Ribbonry
Crazy Rags
Hand-Stitched Samplers from I Done My Best
Miniature Baltimore Album Quilts
A Passion for Ribbonry
A Silk-Ribbon Album
Victorian Elegance

Quiltmaking Basics

Basic Quiltmaking Techniques for Hand Appliqué
Basic Quiltmaking Techniques for Strip Piecing
The Joy of Quilting
A Perfect Match
Press for Success
The Ultimate Book of Quilt Labels
Your First Quilt Book (or it should be!)

Rotary Cutting/Speed Piecing

Around the Block with Judy Hopkins
All-Star Sampler
Bargello Quilts
Block by Block
Down the Rotary Road with Judy Hopkins
Easy Star Sampler
Magic Base Blocks for Unlimited Quilt Designs
A New Slant on Bargello Quilts
Quilting Up a Storm
Rotary Riot
Rotary Roundup
ScrapMania
Simply Scrappy Quilts
Square Dance
Start with Squares
Stripples
Stripples Strikes Again!
Strips that Sizzle
Two-Color Quilts

Seasonal Quilts

Appliquilt® for Christmas
Christmas Ribbonry
Easy Seasonal Wall Quilts
Folded Fabric Fun
Quilted for Christmas
Quilted for Christmas, Book II
Quilted for Christmas, Book III
Quilted for Christmas, Book IV
Welcome to the North Pole

Surface Design/Fabric Manipulation

15 Beads: A Guide to Creating One-of-a-Kind Beads
The Art of Handmade Paper and Collage
Complex Cloth: A Comprehensive Guide
  to Surface Design
Dyes & Paints: A Hands-On Guide to Coloring Fabric
Hand-Dyed Fabric Made Easy

Theme Quilts

The Cat's Meow
Celebrating the Quilt
Class-Act Quilts
The Heirloom Quilt
Honoring the Seasons
Kids Can Quilt
Life in the Country with Country Threads
Lora & Company
Making Memories
More Quilts for Baby
Once Upon a Quilt
Patchwork Pantry
Quick-Sew Celebrations
Quilted Landscapes
Quilted Legends of the West
Quilts: An American Legacy
Quilts for Baby
Quilts from Nature
Through the Window and Beyond
Tropical Punch

Watercolor Quilts

Awash with Colour
Colourwash Quilts
More Strip-Pieced Watercolor Magic
Strip-Pieced Watercolor Magic
Watercolor Impressions
Watercolor Quilts

Wearables

Crazy Rags
Dress Daze
Dressed by the Best
Easy Reversible Vests
Jacket Jazz
More Jazz from Judy Murrah
Quick-Sew Fleece
Sew a Work of Art Inside and Out
Variations in Chenille